A COOK'S TOUR OF FRANCE

Regional French Recipes

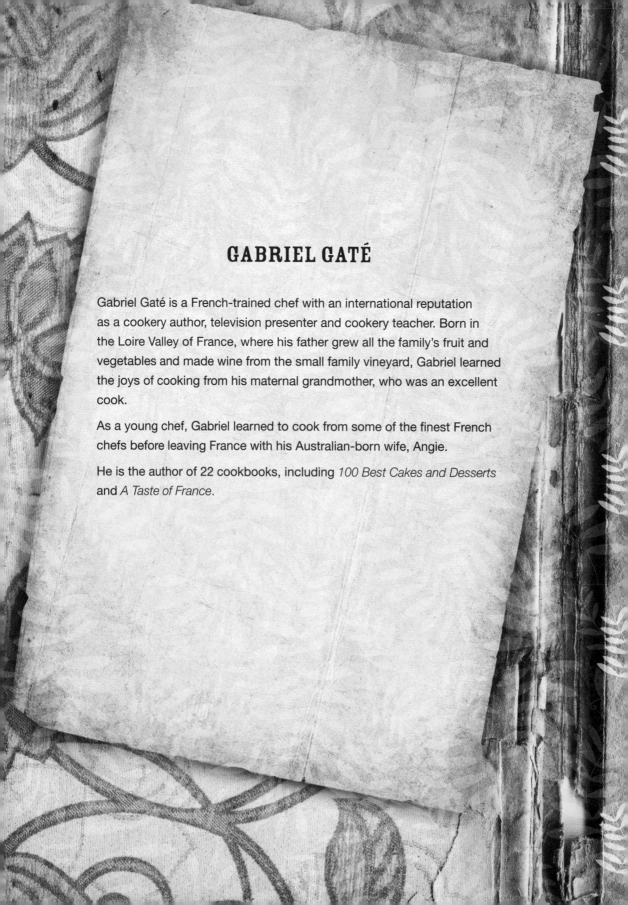

GABRIEL GATÉ

Gabriel Gaté is a French-trained chef with an international reputation as a cookery author, television presenter and cookery teacher. Born in the Loire Valley of France, where his father grew all the family's fruit and vegetables and made wine from the small family vineyard, Gabriel learned the joys of cooking from his maternal grandmother, who was an excellent cook.

As a young chef, Gabriel learned to cook from some of the finest French chefs before leaving France with his Australian-born wife, Angie.

He is the author of 22 cookbooks, including *100 Best Cakes and Desserts* and *A Taste of France*.

A COOK'S TOUR OF

FRANCE

Regional French Recipes

GABRIEL GATÉ

hardie grant books
MELBOURNE · LONDON

An SBS Book

Published in 2015 by Hardie Grant Books

Hardie Grant Books (Australia)
Ground Floor, Building 1
658 Church Street
Richmond, Victoria 3121
www.hardiegrant.com.au

Hardie Grant Books (UK)
5th & 6th Floor
52-54 Southwark Street
London SE1 1RU
www.hardiegrant.co.uk

Cataloguing-in-Publication data is available from the
National Library of Australia.
A Cook's Tour of France
ISBN: 9781743790182

Publisher: Pam Brewster
Cover and text design: Michelle Mackintosh
Typesetting: Pauline Haas
Colour reproduction by Splitting Image Colour Studio
Printed in China by 1010 Printing International Limited

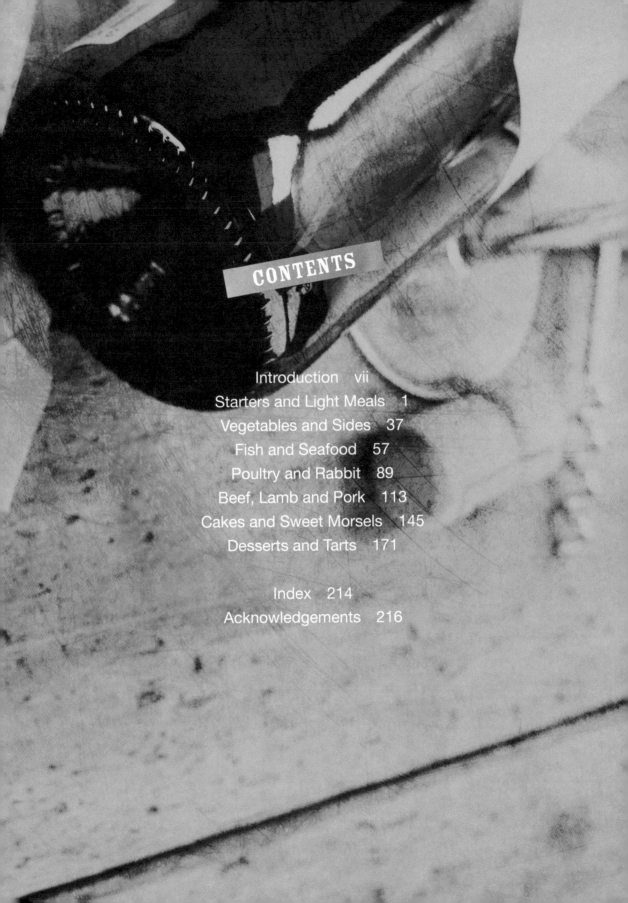

CONTENTS

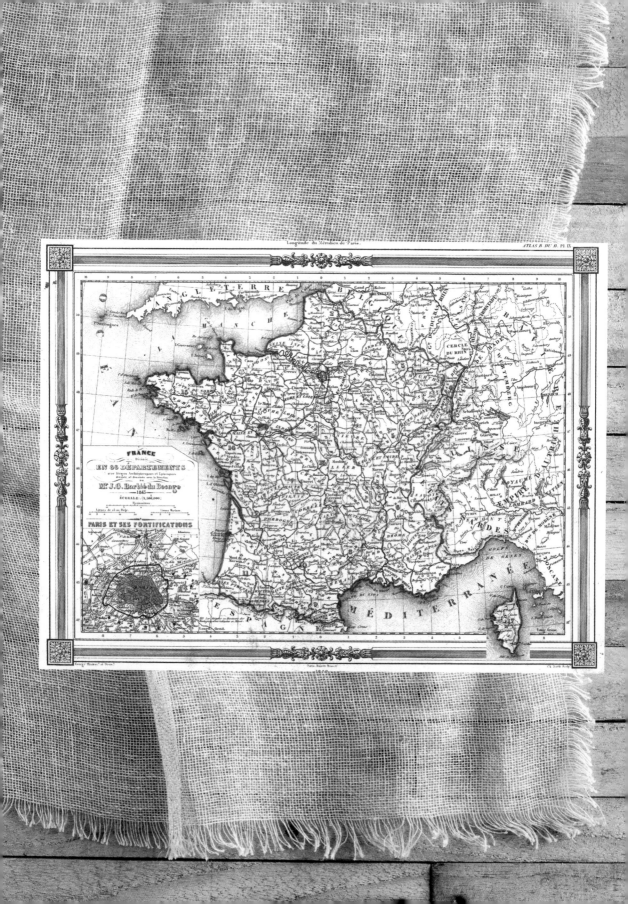

INTRODUCTION

The gastronomy of France is quite simply superb. Its outstanding fish and seafood, excellent wines and liqueurs, extraordinary cheeses, unique range of charcuteries, delicious bread, cakes and pâtisseries are a constant delight for the French people.

Every year in spring, I spend two months travelling in my beloved native land, where I began as a chef more than 40 years ago. During these visits, I produce and present *Taste Le Tour with Gabriel Gaté*, a series of gourmet segments for television, featuring the top specialities of the regions traversed by the amazing Tour de France bicycle race.

Each year the route of the race, which covers about 3500 kilometres (2200 miles) through more than a dozen regions, varies, but it always finishes in Paris on the grand Champs-Elysées boulevard.

This cookbook is a collection of the delicious recipes prepared for the show over the past four years. It includes dishes from all the main regions of France, such as the popular Auge Valley Chicken Casserole from Normandy, the colourful Ratatouille from Nice with Lemon Chantilly and, of course, lovely desserts, as only the French can do, like the luscious Strawberry Tart from the Loire Valley.

I wrote most of the recipes, but a handful of friends, chefs and pastry chefs, in particular Philippe Mouchel and Pierrick Boyer, also contributed.

I hope you derive pleasure from reading these recipes and are inspired to create some special French menus for your family and friends.

Merci et bon appétit.

Gabriel Gaté

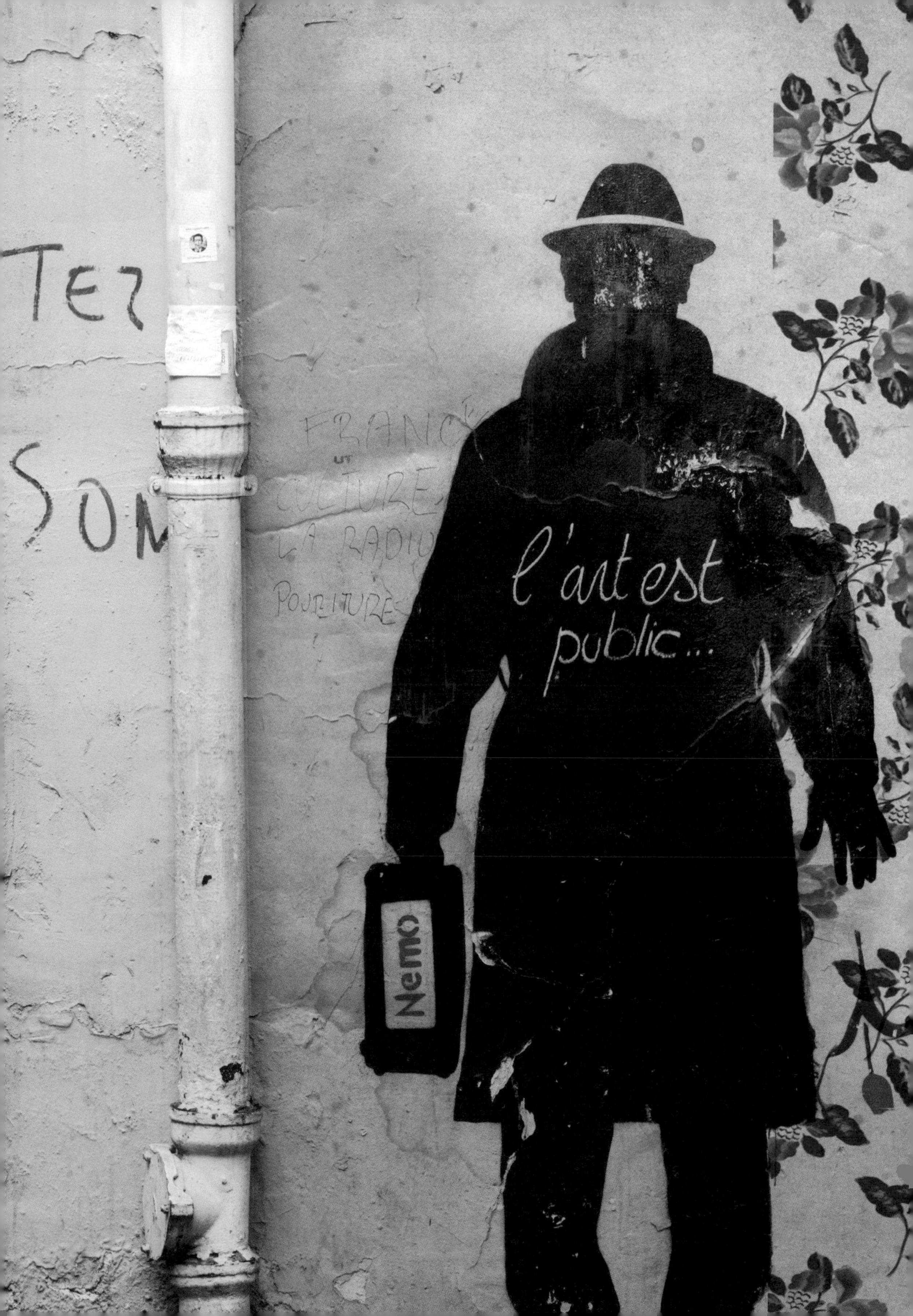
l'art est
public...
Nemo

STARTERS &
LIGHT MEALS

LYONNAISE CHEESE DIP WITH HERBS

Cervelle de Canut
From the Lyonnais-Rhône Alps Region

✦━━━❦❦━━━❦

250 g (8½ oz) creamed cottage cheese or quark (in France it is called *fromage frais*)
50 ml (2 fl oz) crème fraîche
2 tablespoons extra virgin olive oil
1 tablespoon red wine vinegar
1 clove garlic, finely chopped
salt
freshly ground pepper
1 medium shallot, finely chopped
2 tablespoons finely chopped parsley
3 tablespoons finely snipped chives

This dip was created in Lyons, the silk capital of France, in the 19th century, and the French title translates as 'silk worker's brain', meaning it is 'soft'. It's often served with hot baked potatoes but is lovely on toasted sourdough baguette with vegetable sticks.

Place the cottage cheese in a salad bowl and mix in the crème fraîche.

Whisk in the olive oil, vinegar, garlic, salt and pepper, then stir in the shallot, parsley and chives.

Cover with plastic film and refrigerate for 2–3 hours before serving.

SERVES 6-8

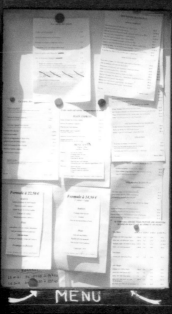

OYSTERS IN CHAMPAGNE SABAYON

Huîtres au sabayon de champagne
From the Champagne Region

50 g (2 oz) butter, melted
1 medium shallot, finely chopped
12 button mushrooms,
finely chopped
salt
freshly ground pepper
12 freshly opened oysters
80 ml (3 fl oz) champagne
2 egg yolks

It's fascinating to visit a champagne cellar in France and then to taste the real thing where it is made. This oyster dish is one of my favourite appetisers.

Preheat the oven to 250°C (480°F/Gas 9).

Heat one-third of the melted butter in a small frying pan. Stir in the shallots and cook on low heat for 2 minutes. Add the chopped mushrooms and cook, stirring occasionally, for about 10 minutes until most of the moisture has evaporated. Season with salt and pepper.

Remove the oysters from the shells and put the shells aside on a baking tray. In a small saucepan, place 50 ml (2 fl oz) of the champagne and bring to a low simmer. Gently stir in the oysters and turn off the heat.

Place the egg yolks and the remaining champagne in a bowl. Place the bowl over a pan of simmering water (bain-marie) and beat the yolks and champagne until light and fluffy. It takes a few minutes and the egg must not scramble.

Remove the bowl from the heat, slowly whisk in the remaining melted butter and season with salt and pepper.

Spoon a little mushroom mixture into each of the 12 oyster shells. Top with a drained oyster, then coat the oysters with the champagne sauce.

Place the oysters in the hot oven for a few minutes until the sauce has lightly browned. Serve immediately.

SERVES 2

POACHED OYSTERS WITH POTATOES & A CHIVE SAUCE

Huîtres pochées sauce ciboulette en pommes de terre
From the Vendée Region

---

6 new potatoes
50 g (2 oz) butter,
cut into small cubes
1 shallot, finely chopped
1 tablespoon white wine vinegar
125 ml (4 ½ fl oz/ ½ cup) dry white wine
freshly ground pepper
1 teaspoon pouring cream
12 freshly opened oysters
2 tablespoons finely snipped chives
a few mixed green salad leaves and herbs

Beautiful beaches and charming fishing ports line the Atlantic coast of the Vendée region. It is known for its seafood, and there are several islands not far from the mainland that produce some of France's finest oysters.

Cook the potatoes in salted boiling water until just done. Drain and peel the potatoes as soon as they can be handled. Place in warm water until ready to use.

Melt 1 teaspoon butter in a small saucepan on medium heat. Stir in the chopped shallot and cook on medium heat for 1 minute. Add the vinegar and about 2 tablespoons white wine. Season with pepper and simmer until the liquid has almost evaporated.

Add the cream to the shallots and bring to a simmer. Whisk in the remaining butter, bit by bit, until creamy. Remove the pan from the heat.

Drain the potatoes. Cut each potato in half and scoop out a teaspoon of flesh from the centre. Remove the oysters from their shells.

Bring the remaining wine to a simmer in a second pan, then gently place the oysters in the pan, discarding the shells, and poach for about 20 seconds. Turn off the heat, drain the oysters and place in the sauce. Add the cut chives.

Divide the 12 potato halves between two plates. Top each potato half with an oyster and spoon over a little sauce. Garnish the plates with a few green leaves and serve.

SERVES 2

BURGUNDY HAM TERRINE

Jambon de Bourgogne persillé
From the Burgundy Region
by Stéphane Langlois

2 litres (68 fl oz/8 cups) pork or
chicken stock
1.3 kg (2 lb 13 oz) salted pork leg,
including some skin
1 litre (34 fl oz/4 cups) clear
chicken stock or water
60 g (2 oz) powdered gelatine
125 ml (4½ fl oz/½ cup) red wine
vinegar
125 ml (4 ½ fl oz/½ cup)
chardonnay or dry white wine
1 brown onion, finely chopped
30 g (½ cup) chopped parsley
ground white pepper

This beautiful ham terrine is a speciality of Burgundy but it is loved all over France. It's usually served as a starter with baguette and gherkins (pickles).

In a stockpot, bring the pork stock to a simmer. Add the pieces of salted pork leg and simmer for about 2 ½ hours. The pork is now ham. Drain the ham, discard the cooking liquid and cool the ham on a dish.

While the ham is cooling down, heat the clear chicken stock in a saucepan and whisk in the gelatine until it has all dissolved. Add the vinegar and wine and allow to cool.

Preheat the oven to 150°C (300°F/Gas 2).

Ladle the chicken stock into a 2-litre (8-cup) terrine dish, enough to cover 1 cm (⅓ in) of its base. Divide the chopped onion and parsley into four and add one-quarter to the dish.

Cut the cooled ham into slices 2 cm (⅔ in) thick and season with a little white pepper. Finely shred the ham skin.

Place a layer of ham on top of the stock in the base of the terrine. Ladle in a bit more stock, then sprinkle with a quarter more onion and parsley and top with the shredded ham skin.

Top with another layer of ham, then ladle in more stock and add a quarter more onion and parsley. Add a final layer of ham and ladle in more stock to cover the ham by about 1 cm (⅓ in). Lastly, top with the remaining onion and parsley.

Place the terrine on a baking tray and into the preheated oven for about 20 minutes.

Remove from the oven and allow to cool, then refrigerate overnight to set.

Turn the terrine out before cutting it into 2 cm (⅔ in) slices.

SERVES ABOUT 10

CANTAL CREAM WITH WILD MUSHROOM TOASTS

Crème de Cantal et son toast de cèpes
From the Auvergne Region
by Francis Delmas

80 g (3 oz) sugar
2 tablespoons water
80 g (3 oz) rhubarb, cut into
1 cm (⅓ in) pieces
1 teaspoon butter
100 ml (3 ½ fl oz) pouring cream
150 g (5 oz) cantal cheese, grated
4 eggs
400 ml (14 fl oz) hot milk
3 tablespoons extra virgin olive oil
200 g (7 oz) cep mushrooms,
sliced
freshly ground pepper
1 clove garlic, finely chopped
100 g (3 ½ oz) extra cantal cheese,
cut into small pieces
6 × 1 cm (⅓ in) thick slices of
baguette, 15 cm (6 in) long
12 cherry tomatoes

Cantal cheese has been made in the mountainous region of Auvergne for more than a thousand years. This wonderful hard cheese, sharp and nutty, resembles a cheddar and is a great cheese to cook with.

Preheat the oven to 140°C (280°F/Gas 1).

In a small saucepan, bring the sugar and water to the boil and cook until it is a light-brown caramel colour.

Pour the caramel into 6 x 100 ml (3 ½ fl oz) porcelain ramekins.

Cook the rhubarb in the butter in a small saucepan until soft, then spoon the rhubarb into the ramekins.

Combine the cream, cheese and eggs in a blender. Add the hot milk and blend again. Pour this custard into the ramekins and place them in a roasting pan. Add enough hot water to the pan to come halfway up the sides of the ramekins.

Cook the custards in the preheated oven for about 20 minutes or until set. Remove from the oven and allow to cool.

Heat half the olive oil in a frying pan and cook the mushrooms for a few minutes. Season with pepper and a little chopped garlic.

Alternate slices of mushroom and cantal cheese on the slices of baguette, then place under a grill and cook until the cheese has melted.

To unmould, run a knife blade around the inside edge of the ramekins and turn the cantal creams out onto plates. Top with a slice of cheese and mushroom toast, garnish with cherry tomatoes and drizzle the remaining olive oil over the top.

SERVES 6

CHEESE FONDUE LES ALPAGES

Fondue les Alpages
From the Alps Region
by Bernard Mure-Ravaud

400 g (14 oz) beaufort cheese
200 g (7 oz) abondance cheese
400 g (14 oz) comté cheese
250 ml (8½ fl oz/1 cup) dry white wine
1 x one-day-old baguette, cut into 1 cm (⅓ in) slices

I had never eaten a great fondue until I tasted this dish prepared by a cheese master using wonderful cheeses. It's easy to make; the secret is to melt the cheese slowly. You will need a cheese fondue set.

Trim the rind of all the cheeses and grate the cheeses very finely. Don't compress the grated cheese.

Place half the wine in a fondue pan on low heat. Add about one-third of the cheese and stir using a wooden spoon as the cheese starts melting.

When the cheese is well on the way to melting, add half the remaining wine and half the remaining cheese, stirring as it continues to melt. Then add the remaining wine and cheese and stir again until it has almost melted.

Lift the cheese slightly from the pan, using a spoon, to give it a bit of elasticity. The cheese is ready when it is stretchy. This is now the fondue.

Do not allow the fondue to boil; it must not become too hot. Keep the fondue warm on a fondue burner.

Cut the baguette slices in half. Attach pieces of bread to fondue forks and dip the bread in the cheese, twisting the fork until the cheese sticks to the bread.

SERVES 4-8

CHEESE & HAM TOASTED SANDWICH

Crôque Monsieur
From the Paris Region
by Philippe Mouchel

8 slices of sandwich bread

8 slices of gruyère cheese, same size as the bread

8 thin slices of ham, same size as the bread

150 g (5 oz) gruyère cheese, grated

100 g (3 ½ oz) parmesan cheese, grated

4 tablespoons pouring cream

2 egg yolks

salt

freshly ground pepper

As a young chef in Paris, I often went out late at night after work to a cabaret and enjoyed a Crôque Monsieur while listening to live music. It smells delicious and is very popular.

Lay out four slices of bread and top each one with a slice of gruyère cheese. Then add a slice of ham, another slice of gruyère and, lastly, another slice of ham.

In a bowl, mix the grated gruyère with the grated parmesan, cream, egg yolks and a little salt and pepper.

Spread the remaining four slices of bread with half of the creamy cheese mixture. Carefully place the bread, cheese-side down, on top of the ham slices. Spread the remaining creamy cheese on top.

Place the Crôque Monsieur on a baking tray and bake in a hot oven or under the grill until the cheese has melted inside and out.

SERVES 4

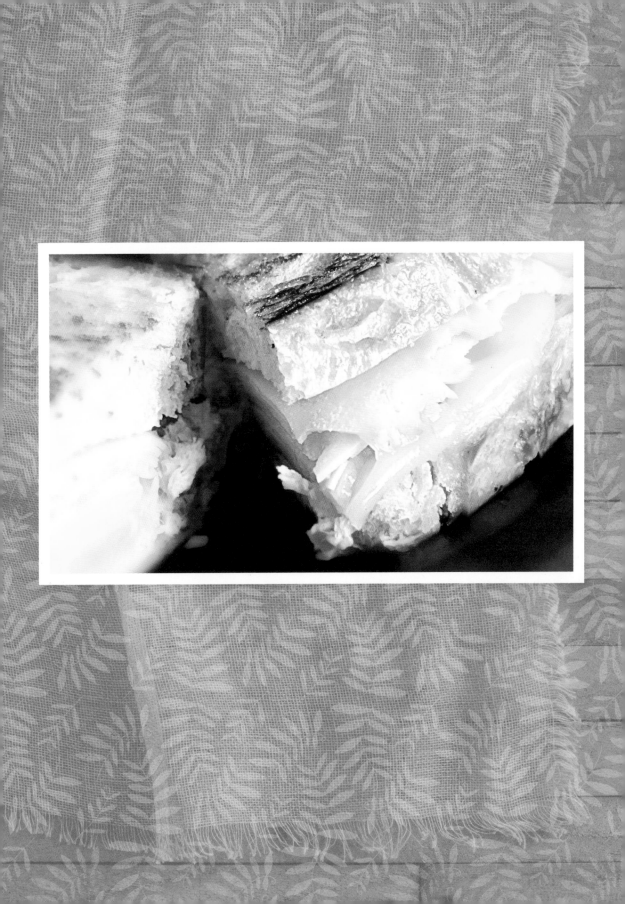

CUCUMBER & SMOKED TROUT TERRINE

Terrine de truite fumée au concombre
From the Savoie/Alps Region

3 long cucumbers
2 tablespoons coarse salt
8 gelatine sheets (or 1 x 7g/¼ oz sachet powdered gelatine)
salt
freshly ground pepper
½ cup (30 g) finely chopped dill
250 ml (8½ fl oz/1 cup) crème fraîche
a little extra virgin olive oil
2 eggs, hard-boiled
3 smoked trout fillets, skinned and boneless

Trout fishing and trout eating are popular activities in the alpine region where lakes, rivers and streams abound. This extremely light terrine is ideal as a first course for a special dinner party.

I use a 24 cm (10 in) ring tin to mould the terrine.

Peel the cucumbers, then cut them in four lengthways. Remove the seeds and cut the cucumber into thin slices. Place in a bowl, toss with the coarse salt and put aside for 1 hour.

Place the gelatine sheets in a large bowl of cold water to soften for about 10 minutes.

Rinse and drain the cucumber. Pat it dry with paper towels or a clean tea towel. Blend the cucumber to a coarse purée, place in a bowl and season with pepper. Mix in the chopped dill.

Warm the crème fraîche in a small saucepan. Drain the softened gelatine sheets, squeezing them by hand to remove excess water, then add the gelatine sheets (or the powdered gelatine) to the warm crème fraîche, stirring to dissolve. Add this to the cucumber and mix well.

Brush the inside of the ring tin with olive oil and line the base with finely cut slices of hard-boiled egg. I use an egg slicer for more even results.

Pour about one-third of the cucumber preparation into the tin. Top with half of the trout fillets and another third of the cucumber mixture. Top with the remaining trout fillets and cucumber mixture.

Cover with plastic film and refrigerate for at least 6 hours.

Unmould the terrine carefully by dipping the mould briefly in hot water. Cut the terrine into 6 cm (2 in) slices and serve.

SERVES ABOUT 10

DUCK BALLOTINE

Ballotine de canard
From the Vendée Region
by Philippe Mouchel

---

600 g (1 lb 5 oz) duck leg meat, minced (ground)
150 g (5 oz) duck breast, diced
150 g (5 oz) veal, diced
150 g (5 oz) pork fat, minced (ground)
50 g (2 oz) pistachio nuts
30 ml (1 fl oz) madeira
30 ml (1 fl oz) cognac
120 ml (4 fl oz) dry white wine
salt
freshly ground pepper
1 teaspoon four-spice mix
1 duck, deboned
300 g (10 oz) foie gras, cut into 2 cm (⅔ in) chunks
1 litre (34 fl oz/4 cups) duck or chicken stock
gherkins (pickles)
green salad
vegetable pickles

For this sophisticated terrine-style dish you will need a deboned duck. If you are not sure how to do it, ask your poultry supplier to debone it for you.

In a bowl, thoroughly combine the minced duck leg with the diced duck breast, veal, pork fat, pistachio nuts, madeira, cognac, dry white wine, a little salt and pepper and the four-spice mix. Cover and refrigerate overnight. This mixture is called forcemeat.

Place the deboned duck, skin-side down, on several layers of plastic wrap. Spread the duck forcemeat on top of the deboned duck, leaving about 2 cm (⅔ in) at the edge free of forcemeat.

Position the foie gras chunks lengthways along the centre, from the duck neck to the tail end of the duck. Carefully, but firmly, roll the deboned duck to enclose the forcemeat and foie gras. Then firmly wrap the duck parcel (ballotine) in the plastic wrap, securing the ends and centre with kitchen string.

In a large saucepan, bring the stock to almost a simmer, then immerse the ballotine into the stock to poach for about 2 hours. It's best if it does not boil.

Allow the ballotine to completely cool in the liquid, then refrigerate it.

Cut the ballotine into slices about 1 cm (⅓ in) thick and serve with gherkins (pickles), a little green salad drizzled with olive oil and some vegetable pickles.

SERVES 6-8

DUCK SALAD
WITH GREEN BEANS
& FOIE GRAS

*Salade de canard aux haricots
verts et au foie gras*
From the South West Region

2 boneless duck fillets, skin on
salt
freshly ground black pepper
1 tablespoon extra virgin olive oil
150 g (5 oz) green beans, topped
and tailed
1 tablespoon red wine vinegar
3 tablespoons walnut oil
½ shallot, finely chopped
1 tablespoon chopped walnuts
1 tablespoon finely snipped chives
8 cherry tomatoes, halved
2 tablespoons foie gras, cut into
small squares

*This type of gourmet French salad was served in the
top restaurants forty years ago when I was working
as a young chef. It's simple to prepare and so refined
especially if you can get some good quality foie gras.*

Preheat the oven to 100°C (210°F/Gas ¼).

Season the duck fillets with salt and pepper.

Heat the olive oil in an ovenproof frying pan on medium heat
then cook the duck fillets, skin-side down, for 2 minutes. Turn
the duck fillets over then place in the preheated oven to roast
for about 12 minutes.

Remove the duck from the oven and allow to rest and cool for
about 15 minutes.

Meanwhile, cook the green beans in a saucepan of salted
boiling water until just done. Drain the beans and cool in cold
water, then drain again.

Place a pinch of salt and a little black pepper in a bowl. Mix in
the red wine vinegar and walnut oil. Stir in the chopped shallot,
walnuts and half the chives. Add the halved cherry tomatoes
and the beans and mix gently.

Thinly slice the duck fillets and arrange in a circle on the plate.
Spoon the bean salad into the centre and top with the foie gras
squares.

Sprinkle with the remaining chives and serve.

SERVES 2

GOURMET YABBY SALAD WITH PEARS & WALNUTS

Salade gourmande d'écrevisses
aux poires et aux noix
From the Dauphinée/Alps Region

—⚜——⟆——⚘—

about 28 cooked yabbies
½ tablespoon red wine vinegar
juice of ½ lemon
salt
freshly ground black pepper
3 tablespoons walnut oil
1 shallot, finely chopped
100 g (3 ½ oz) cooked baby
green beans, cooled
1 cup (3 ½ oz/45 g) mixed green
salad leaves
½ cup (2 oz/60 g) walnut halves
1 pear, just ripe

This is an outstanding starter, especially if you can source fresh yabbies. They have a uniquely delicate and sweet flavour of yabbies and are a popular dish served in the top French restaurants of the Alps region. If yabbies are not available, try prawns or scampi.

Shell, devein and clean the yabbies.

In a bowl mix together the red wine vinegar, lemon juice, a little salt, pepper, walnut oil and chopped shallot.

Add the green beans, the mixed green leaves, the walnut halves and the yabbies and mix gently together.

Halve and core the pear and slice thinly.

Form a circle of the pear slices in the centre of each plate. Gently spoon the salad on top of the pear slices and serve.

SERVES 4

PORTA
SENESE

LEEK TART

Flamiche aux poireaux
From the Northern France/
Belgium Region

1 tablespoon vegetable oil
150 g (5 oz) bacon, diced
30 g (1 oz) butter
3 medium leeks, white part only,
thinly sliced
400 g (14 oz) savoury shortcrust
pastry
4 large eggs
100 ml (3 ½ fl oz) milk
150 ml (5 fl oz) pouring cream
salt
freshly ground pepper

*Leeks are one of the most loved vegetables in France
and the cool climate of northern France is perfect for
their cultivation. This is my favourite savoury tart.*

Preheat the oven to 220°C (430°F/Gas 7). You will need a
25 cm (9 in) loose-based flan (tart) tin.

Heat the oil in a wide non-stick pan and brown the bacon in it
for 2–3 minutes. Transfer the bacon to a bowl.

Add the butter and the leeks to the pan and cook on low heat
for 10–15 minutes until the leeks are soft, stirring occasionally
with a wooden spoon. Allow the leeks to cool.

Roll out the pastry to a thickness of about 4 mm (⅙ in). Line
the tin with the pastry and prick the pastry about 30 times with
a fork.

Spread the cold leeks and bacon over the pastry.

In a bowl, whisk together the eggs, milk and cream. Season
with salt and pepper, then carefully pour the mixture over
the leeks and bacon.

Place the tin on a baking tray and bake in the preheated oven
for about 40 minutes until the pastry is cooked and filling set.
Serve hot.

SERVES 6-8

HERRING SALAD WITH POTATOES

Salade de harengs aux pommes de terre
From the Northern France Region
by Philippe Mouchel

salt
freshly ground pepper
1 tablespoon red wine vinegar
1 teaspoon dijon mustard
3 tablespoons vegetable oil
450–500 g (1 lb–1 lb 2 oz) cooked potatoes in their skins (kipflers are great)
1 tablespoon dry white wine
1 large shallot, finely chopped
2 tablespoons chopped parsley
2 tablespoons finely chopped tarragon leaves
4 herring fillets, marinated in oil and vegetables

Forty years ago this was a popular salad served in working-class French restaurants. Marinated herring fillets in oil were an easy dish to prepare and it made a tasty, satisfying salad for workers. You'll find herring in oil in European-style delicatessens and gourmet stores.

In a bowl, mix together a little salt and pepper, the vinegar, mustard and oil to make a dressing.

Peel and slice the cooked potatoes. While they are still warm, mix them with the wine, then mix in the chopped shallot, dressing, chopped parsley and tarragon.

Spoon a little potato salad onto each plate then top with a herring fillet and a little vegetable garnish from the marinade. Season with a bit more black pepper and serve.

SERVES 4

LIÈGEOISE SALAD WITH MUSSELS

Salade Liègeoise aux moules
From the Northern France/Belgium
Region

2 medium all-purpose potatoes
200 g (7 oz) green beans
500 g (1 lb 2 oz) mussels, cleaned
30 ml (1 oz) dry white wine or beer
salt
freshly ground pepper
2 rashers of bacon, diced
1 tablespoon extra virgin olive oil
1 shallot, finely chopped
½ small brown onion, finely
chopped
2 tablespoons red wine vinegar
3 tablespoons chopped parsley
2 tablespoons finely snipped chives

A delicious potato, bean and bacon salad, it is very popular in the north of France and originally a speciality of Liège. Here I serve it with mussels, which the French adore. It can also be served on its own or with grilled meat or fish, and makes a lovely summer starter.

In a saucepan, boil the potatoes in their skins until cooked, then drain. Add the beans to a saucepan of boiling water and continue boiling until cooked. Drain and refresh in cold water.

Place the mussels and the wine in a large saucepan, cover with a lid and bring to the boil. The mussels will open and be cooked in a few minutes. Shake the pan a few times during the cooking.

When all the mussels are open, drain the liquid and remove the mussels from the shells.

Peel and cube the potatoes, place in a bowl with the cooked beans and season with a little salt and pepper.

Cook the diced bacon in a non-stick pan for a few minutes, then transfer to a plate.

Add the olive oil to the pan and cook the chopped shallot and onion until soft and lightly browned. Stir in the vinegar and briefly bring to the boil. Add the cooked onion to the potatoes and beans and combine, then gently mix in the bacon and chopped parsley.

Season the mussels with pepper and chives.

Place a little of the Liègeoise salad on each plate, arrange the mussels around the salad and serve.

SERVES 2

SNAILS IN GARLIC & WALNUT BUTTER

Escargots au beurre d'ail et de noix
From the Midi-Pyrénées Region

150 g (5 oz) butter, softened
1 shallot, finely chopped
2 cloves garlic, finely chopped
3 tablespoons finely chopped parsley
80 g (3 oz) walnuts, finely chopped
salt
freshly ground pepper
1 tablespoon lemon juice
48 cooked snails, rinsed and drained
600 g (1 lb 5oz) baby spinach leaves, washed
4 tablespoons pouring cream
4 tablespoons dried breadcrumbs

For the French this is a very festive dish and each region has its own version – but they all contain lots of garlic. In the Midi-Pyrénées region walnuts are added for an extra crunch.

Preheat the oven to 180°C (350°F/Gas 4).

In a bowl, combine the softened butter, chopped shallot, garlic, parsley and walnuts. Season with salt, pepper and lemon juice. Place the mixture between two sheets of baking paper and roll into a square 5 mm (¼ in) thick. Cover in plastic wrap and place in the freezer to chill.

Place the spinach in a pot, cover with a lid and cook until just wilted. Drain the spinach and squeeze out the excess water.

Heat the cream in a pan. Stir in the spinach and season with salt and pepper.

Transfer the spinach to four individual gratin dishes and top each with 12 snails.

Remove the walnut butter from the freezer. Cut into four squares and place a piece on each serve of snails. Sprinkle breadcrumbs on top. Cook in the preheated oven for 10 minutes until hot. Serve immediately.

SERVES 4

VEGETABLES
& SIDES

BELGIAN WITLOF GRATIN

Endives au gratin
From the Northern France/Belgium Region

———⋯———

4 medium witlof (chicory/Belgian endive)
80 g (3 oz) butter,
cut into small pieces
salt
freshly ground pepper
4 tablespoons chopped parsley
50 g (2 oz) plain (all-purpose) flour
500 ml (18 fl oz/2 cups) milk
a pinch of grated nutmeg
a pinch of cayenne pepper
120 g (4 oz) gruyère cheese,
grated
4–8 thin slices of ham

This speciality of northern France is a popular winter dish that my mother would prepare every week for dinner for our family as a main meal. I remember not liking the bitterness of the witlof at first. I love it now.

Preheat the oven to 220°C (430°F/Gas 7).

Remove any damaged witlof leaves and trim the hard ends, keeping each witlof in one piece.

Place about 20 g (⅔ oz) butter in a small saucepan. Add the witlof on top and season with salt and pepper. Sprinkle 2 tablespoons chopped parsley over the top and cover with a layer of baking paper. Place on low heat and cook for 20–25 minutes, turning the witlof several times during the cooking. Transfer the cooked witlof to a plate and leave to cool slightly.

Melt the remaining butter in a saucepan on medium heat. Whisk in the plain flour and cook for 2–3 minutes. Bit by bit, whisk in the cold milk until you obtain a smooth sauce. Cook for 2 minutes and season with salt, pepper, nutmeg and cayenne pepper and stir in 80 g (3 oz) grated gruyère cheese.

When the witlof is cool enough to handle, wrap each one in a slice or two of ham. Place in a greased gratin dish and spoon the sauce over the top. Sprinkle with the remaining chopped parsley and remaining gruyère.

Place in the preheated oven and cook for 10–15 minutes until golden brown. Take care, it's very hot!

SERVES 4

POTATO & REBLOCHON CHEESE GRATIN

Tartiflette au reblochon
From the Haute Savoie/Alps Region

⊰━━⟩⟩⟩━━⊱

20 g (¾ oz) butter
2 brown onions, thinly sliced
250 g (8½ oz) smoked bacon, diced
1.5 kg (3 lb 5 oz) all-purpose potatoes, cooked in their skins and cut in 1 cm (⅓ in) slices
salt
freshly ground pepper
3 tablespoons crème fraîche
1 reblochon cheese, cut in half horizontally and then in half vertically (or 450 g/1 lb of another washed-rind cheese)
125 ml (4½ fl oz/½ cup) dry white wine
2 tablespoons chopped parsley

This tasty gratin-style dish, often served in the alpine ski resorts, is a wonderful choice for a winter dinner and a popular party dish for young adults.

Preheat the oven to 180°C (350°F/Gas 4).

Heat the butter in a frying pan and cook the onion for 3–4 minutes. Add the bacon and cook for a few more minutes before adding the potatoes. Stir well, season with salt and pepper and cook for about 5 minutes.

Butter a large gratin dish. Line the base of the dish with the potato preparation. Spoon the crème fraîche on top and finish with a layer of cheese. Pour the wine down the side of the dish.

Bake in the preheated oven for about 10 minutes or until it bubbles and the cheese has just melted.

Serve sprinkled with a little chopped parsley.

SERVES 8-10

POTATO PURÉE WITH CHEESE

Aligot
From the South Auvergne Region
by Nicolas Poelaert

———

250 g (8½ oz) potatoes (desirée
are good)
40 g (1½ oz) butter
50 ml (2 fl oz) thickened cream
90 g (3 oz) strong-flavoured
melting cow's milk cheese, such
as gruyère, thinly sliced or grated
(Nicolas used a Tomme cow's
milk cheese)

Thirty years ago this dish was really only known in the south of the mountainous region of Auvergne, but now that the world has gone crazy about mashed potato it's become very fashionable to serve aligot at foodie dinners all around the world.

Peel and quarter the potatoes. Place the potatoes in a saucepan filled with cold salted water and boil until tender.

Drain the potatoes and push them through a mouli into a saucepan, add the butter and cream.

Place the pan on a medium heat and, using a wooden spoon, stir in the cheese, stirring in one direction until the cheese has melted and the purée is elastic and stretches like a dough.

Aligot is often served with prosciutto-style ham and a green salad.

SERVES 2-3

RATATOUILLE WITH LEMON CHANTILLY

Verrine de ratatouille
Niçoise au chantilly citron
From the Nice/Riviera Region

4 tablespoons extra virgin olive oil
1 small onion, diced
1 tablespoon chopped thyme
1 clove garlic, chopped
1 red capsicum (pepper), diced
1 green capsicum (pepper), diced
1 medium eggplant (aubergine),
diced
1 medium zucchini (courgette),
diced
salt
freshly ground pepper
3 tomatoes
250 ml (8½ fl oz/1 cup) crème
fraîche
juice of ½ lemon
2 tablespoons pitted black olives,
diced
6 niçoise olives
(small, like ligurian olives)

Popular both in France and around the world, ratatouille is a speciality of the Mediterranean city of Nice.

Heat the olive oil in a saucepan. Add the onion and thyme and stir on medium heat for 2 minutes. Stir in the chopped garlic, the red and green capsicums and cook for a few minutes. Add the eggplant, stir for a few minutes, then add the zucchini. Stir well and season with salt and pepper.

Halve the tomatoes and squeeze out the seeds. Discard the tomato seeds, dice the flesh and add to the other vegetables. Stir well and simmer for about 15 minutes or until the vegetables are soft. Transfer to a bowl, allow to cool and refrigerate when cold.

In a bowl, season the crème fraîche with salt and pepper and whip until almost firm. Add the lemon juice and continue whipping until the chantilly is firm.

Transfer the ratatouille into six glasses. Top with the diced, pitted olives, pipe the cream on top and garnish with an olive.

SERVES 6

SAVOY POTATO GRATIN

Gratin Savoyard
From the Alps Region

1.5 kg (3 lb 5 oz) all-purpose
potatoes of regular shape
(desiree are good)
salt
freshly ground pepper
nutmeg, grated
80 g (3 oz) butter
150 g (5 oz) gruyère cheese,
grated
150 g (5 oz) beaufort cheese,
grated
375 ml (13 fl oz/1½ cups) chicken
stock

I am a cheese lover and the cheeses from the Alps really satisfy me with their beautiful nutty flavour. The local gruyère and beaufort are great cooking cheeses, and in this classic gratin savoyard cheese is the star.

Alpine families love this classic potato dish, which is very easy to make and delicious. It's usually served at dinner with a salad or at Sunday lunch as part of a feast.

Preheat the oven to 200°C (400°F/Gas 6).

Peel the potatoes, cut them into 3 mm (⅛ in) slices and place in a bowl with salt, pepper and a little grated nutmeg. Mix well together.

Generously grease a medium to large ovenproof gratin dish with one-third of the butter. Place half the potato slices neatly in the dish and top with the grated gruyère cheese. Cover with the remaining potatoes, taking time to make a regular pattern with the slices. Sprinkle the beaufort cheese on top and dot with knobs of the remaining butter.

Carefully pour the chicken stock into the dish.

Bake in the preheated oven for 15 minutes, then lower the heat to 150°C (300°F/Gas 2) and cook for a further 45 minutes or until the potatoes are soft.

SERVES 6-8

BABY BEETROOT WITH BURNED CARROT PURÉE

*Petites betteraves à la purée
de carottes brûlées*
From the Northern France Region
by Nicolas Poelaert

⊰ ⟶ ⊱

2 medium carrots
salt
freshly ground pepper
2 tablespoons extra virgin olive oil
8 baby beetroot (beets)
10 g (⅓ oz) butter
a selection of herbs and flowers
from the garden; e.g. chervil,
tarragon, parsley

*In the north of France, beetroot and other root
vegetables are grown. They have gained enormous
popularity in the last 20 years and this delicious dish
is a good example of modern French cuisine.*

Place the carrots on a grill plate or under the grill to burn the
skin off. When the skin is dark, put the carrots in a steamer and
cook until tender.

Transfer the carrots to a blender, season with salt, pepper and
the olive oil and blend to a very smooth purée. The purée will
be very dark and have a smoky flavour.

Wash the beetroot well and trim the leaves and roots. Cook
beetroot in salted boiling water until tender. Peel and quarter
the beetroot.

Heat the butter in a saucepan and toss the beetroot in
the butter.

Spread a little carrot purée on each plate. Top with the beetroot
pieces and garnish with the herbs and flowers.

SERVES 2

BAKED HARICOT BEANS WITH SMOKED BACON

Haricots blancs des
Pyrénées au lard fumé
From the Pyrénées Region

¾ cup (150 g/5 oz) dried haricot
beans
½ onion, sliced
2 cloves garlic, crushed
2 sprigs of thyme, chopped
100 g (3½ oz) smoked bacon
1 spicy Spanish-style sausage
1 tablespoon extra virgin olive oil
1 teaspoon tomato paste
(concentrated paste)
2 tablespoons dry white wine
30 g (1 oz) butter
2 tablespoons chopped parsley
1 clove extra garlic,
finely chopped
freshly ground black pepper

This lovely baked bean recipe, cooked with charcuterie like tasty bacon and sausage to boost the flavour, is a perfect example of a traditional French family dish.

Place the dried haricot beans in a bowl. Cover with plenty of cold water and soak overnight.

Drain the beans, place in a saucepan and cover with cold water. Add the onion, crushed garlic and thyme and bring to the boil. Simmer for about 1 hour until the beans are tender.

Drain the cooked beans and discard the onion and garlic.

Cut the bacon and sausage into slices 1 cm (⅓ in) thick.

Heat the olive oil in a frying pan and cook the bacon for 1 minute. Add the sausage and cook for 2 minutes. Stir in the tomato paste, the beans and white wine and cook gently for a few minutes.

Stir in the butter, chopped parsley and extra garlic and season with black pepper.

SERVES 2-3

FISH & SEAFOOD

BAKED GURNARD & FENNEL PURÉE

Grondin rôti à la
purée de fenouil
From the Marseille/Provence Region

4 tablespoons extra virgin olive oil
1 shallot, finely chopped
2 cloves garlic, chopped
2 small fennel bulbs,
each cut into 4 wedges
2 sprigs of parsley
2 sprigs of thyme
2 tablespoons pernod
4 tablespoons dry white wine
a pinch of saffron
2 tomatoes, chopped
salt
freshly ground pepper
350 g (12 oz) gurnard fillets
2 tablespoons chopped parsley

The capital of Provence, Marseille, is famous for its seafood cuisine which is wonderfully colourful and flavoursome. Flathead, john dory or monkfish could also be used in this dish.

Preheat the oven to 140°C (280°F/Gas 1).

Heat half the olive oil in an ovenproof dish. Stir in the shallots and garlic, then add the fennel wedges and cook for 2 minutes. Add the parsley and thyme and stir well. Add the pernod and wine and bring to the boil. Add the saffron and tomatoes and season with salt and pepper. Stir well and simmer for 5 minutes.

Top with the fish fillets, drizzle the remaining olive oil over the fish and bake in the preheated oven for about 5 minutes or until the fish is almost cooked. Transfer the fish to a warm plate and cover with foil.

Remove the fennel wedges from the dish and blend them to a purée. Strain the tomato sauce.

Spoon a little of the fennel purée onto each plate. Top with a fish fillet and coat with the tomato sauce. Sprinkle with parsley and serve.

SERVES 2

BAKED TROUT WITH HERBS & BACON

Truite rôtie aux herbes et lardons
From the Midi-Pyrénées Region

1 trout, about 1 kg (2 lb 3 oz),
cleaned and scaled
6 tablespoons extra virgin olive oil
4 sprigs of thyme, finely chopped
salt
freshly ground pepper
2 bay leaves
3 cloves garlic
3 thin slices of lemon
½ apple, peeled, cored and
cut into 3 mm (⅛ in) cubes
8 walnut halves, finely chopped
juice of ½ lemon
3 rashers of bacon, cut into
small strips
3 tablespoons finely snipped chives

The streams of the Pyrénées teem with trout that can be seen swimming in the water from the river bank. I've adapted this classic baked trout recipe by adding small apple cubes and walnuts. It's superb.

Preheat the oven to 140°C (280°F/Gas 1).

Pat the trout dry with paper towel and place on a baking tray lined with baking paper.

In a bowl, mix 3 tablespoons of the olive oil with the chopped thyme and a little salt and pepper. Brush the inside and outside of the trout with this flavoured oil.

Insert the bay leaves, whole garlic cloves and lemon slices inside the fish. Place the fish in the preheated oven for about 30 minutes or until cooked, basting occasionally to keep the fish moist.

Meanwhile, mix together in a bowl the remaining oil, diced apple, chopped walnuts, lemon juice and season with salt and pepper.

Just before the trout is ready, cook the bacon for a few minutes in a small frying pan.

Carefully transfer the trout to a serving platter. Spoon a little of the apple and walnut preparation on top, sprinkle with bacon pieces and chives and serve.

SERVES 4

BRITTANY FISH STEW

Cotriade
From the Brittany Region

⊰——⬢——⊱

80 g (3 oz) butter
1 onion, chopped
1 leek, chopped
2 cloves garlic, chopped
3 sprigs of thyme
6 medium all-purpose potatoes,
peeled and quartered
1 litre (34 fl oz/4 cups) cold water
salt
freshly ground pepper
1½ kg (3 lb 5 oz) whole fishes
(e.g. monkfish, flathead, john dory,
whiting), cleaned and cut into 3 cm
(1 in) pieces
12 mussels, scrubbed and beards
removed
4 tablespoons chopped parsley

Cotriade is a traditional coastal Breton fish and potato soup and every family has their own recipe. It's made using whole fish, cut into pieces rather than fillets, and it is best to include at least three different types of fish.

Gently heat the butter in a large saucepan. Add the onion and stir for 2 minutes. Add the leek and garlic and stir for a further 2 minutes. Add the thyme and potatoes and stir for another minute. Cover with the litre of cold water, season with salt and pepper, bring to the boil and cook for 5 minutes.

Add the fish pieces and shake the saucepan. Simmer for about 5 minutes.

Add the mussels, cover with a lid and cook for 2–3 minutes until the mussels have opened.

Serve the stew in large bowls and sprinkle with parsley.

SERVES 4

CORSICAN CRAYFISH WITH LINGUINI

Langouste de Corse aux linguine
From the Corsica Region

1 cooked crayfish, about 800 g
(1 lb 12 oz)
4 tablespoons extra virgin olive oil
1 onion, finely chopped
10 fennel seeds
10 cumin seeds
1 small chilli, cut in half lengthways,
seeds removed
1 teaspoon tomato paste
(concentrated purée)
1 teaspoon plain (all-purpose) flour
1 teaspoon brandy
75 ml (2½ fl oz) dry white wine
3 tomatoes, diced
salt
freshly ground pepper
150 g (5 oz) linguini
6 basil leaves
½ clove garlic, chopped

The Corsicans, whose island is in the middle of the Mediterranean Sea, are very fond of seafood and crustaceans. They are skilled fishermen and their recipes are richly flavoured. They call crayfish the 'queen of crustaceans'.

Remove the meat from the crayfish legs and body and cut the body meat into bite-size pieces. Refrigerate until required. Cut the shells into small pieces.

Heat half the olive oil in a heavy medium saucepan. Add the crayfish shells and onion and cook on medium heat, stirring for a few minutes. Stir in the fennel and cumin seeds and the chilli, then add the tomato paste and flour. Stir well. Add the brandy and wine and stir until the liquid is combined.

Stir in the tomatoes, season with salt and pepper and simmer for 15 minutes. Then strain the sauce into a saucepan.

Cook the pasta in boiling salted water for a few minutes, then drain.

Heat the crayfish meat in the sauce for a few minutes.

Chop the basil leaves and mix them in a bowl with the remaining olive oil and the chopped garlic.

Place half the linguini on each plate and top with the crayfish meat and sauce. Drizzle with the basil olive oil and serve.

SERVES 2

CRAYFISH GRATIN

Langouste gratinée
From the Languedoc-Roussillon Region

2 x 700 g (1 lb 9 oz) cooked crayfish
80 g (3 oz) butter
2 shallots, finely chopped
2 tablespoons plain (all-purpose) flour
100 ml (3½ fl oz) dry white wine
500 ml (17 fl oz/2 cups) milk
salt
freshly ground pepper
a pinch of cayenne pepper
4 tablespoons parmesan, grated or gruyère cheese
50 g (2 oz/½ cup) fine breadcrumbs

The coast around the Languedoc-Roussillon region abounds in superb shellfish and this crayfish gratin is a famous French classic. It's fairly easy to prepare but make sure the crayfish is freshly cooked and has not been frozen.

Preheat the oven to 220°C (430°F/Gas 7).

Cut each cooked crayfish in half lengthways. You can ask your fishmonger to do it for you if you prefer. Carefully remove the flesh from the tail. Detach and discard the intestine. Dice the flesh into 1½ cm (⅔ in) squares and refrigerate until required.

Place the four half-crayfish shells in a gratin dish for later.

Heat half the butter in a small saucepan. Add the shallots and stir until almost golden. Stir in the flour and cook on low heat for a few minutes.

Whisk in the white wine. When it is well incorporated, gradually whisk in the milk and cook on low heat for 5 minutes. Season with salt, pepper and cayenne pepper.

Gently mix in the crayfish pieces and the parmesan and heat for 2 minutes.

Spoon the crayfish and sauce into the empty crayfish shells. Sprinkle the top evenly with breadcrumbs and dot a little of the remaining butter here and there. Place in the preheated oven and brown the top of the crayfish. It will take about 10 minutes. Serve immediately.

SERVES 4

FISH STEW FROM DIEPPE

Marmite Dieppoise
From the Normandy Region

16 mussels, scrubbed and beards removed
30 ml (1 fl oz) dry white wine
50 g (2 oz) butter
1 leek, white part only, thinly sliced
½ onion, finely chopped
1 celery stalk, diced
50 ml (2 fl oz) dry apple cider
600 g (1 lb 5 oz) firm fish fillets;
e.g. monkfish, flathead
8–12 prawns, shelled and deveined
12 scallops
125 ml (4 ½ fl oz/½ cup) cream
salt
freshly ground pepper
12 sprigs of chervil

Normandy is synonymous with outstanding seafood. The French really know how to handle fish and love to eat it. It's not uncommon for a small coastal village to have two or three seafood shops selling the local catch. This seafood stew is named after the fishing town of Dieppe.

Place the cleaned mussels in a saucepan with the dry white wine, cover with a lid and bring to the boil. The mussels will open after a few minutes. Shake the mussels around and when they are all open, strain the liquid into a bowl. Remove the mussels from the shells and place in the mussel juice.

Heat the butter in a wide saucepan on medium heat and cook the leeks, onion and celery for a few minutes until soft. Pour in the apple cider and bring to the boil. Place the fish fillets, prawns and scallops on top and add the mussel juice. Cover with baking paper to keep in the juices and simmer for a few minutes until the fish is just cooked.

Carefully lift the cooked fish and seafood onto individual warm plates or a warm platter.

Add the cream to the pan and bring to the boil, cooking until the sauce thickens. Season with salt and pepper, then stir in the mussels, reheating for a few seconds.

Coat the fish and seafood with the sauce and mussels, garnish with sprigs of chervil and serve.

SERVES 4

JOHN DORY WITH ASPARAGUS & A CHAMPAGNE SAUCE

St Pierre aux asperges sauce champagne
From the Champagne Region
by Philippe Mouchel

—◦◦◦◦—

50 g (2 oz) mushrooms, sliced
1 shallot, finely sliced
40 g (1½ oz) butter
6 sprigs of parsley
2 sprigs of thyme
2 x 180 g (6 oz) john dory fillets
salt
freshly ground black pepper
150 ml (5 fl oz) French champagne
2 teaspoons extra virgin olive oil
6 asparagus spears, trimmed and peeled
125 ml (4 ½ fl oz/½ cup) thickened cream
about 10 tarragon leaves

Every French chef learns to make a champagne sauce and I vividly recall the first time I made one – as a young chef working in a seafood restaurant in Paris. It's a lovely sauce to serve with fish. Only a little champagne is used in the sauce, so you can drink what's left over!

Preheat the oven to 170°C (340°F/Gas 3).

Place the sliced mushrooms in an ovenproof pan with the sliced shallot, a quarter of the butter, the parsley and thyme. Top with the john dory fillets, season with salt and pepper and pour over the champagne.

On top of the stove, bring the pan to a simmer then cover with a lid and put into the preheated oven to bake for about 10 minutes.

Heat the olive oil and half the remaining butter in a pan and cook the asparagus for about 1 minute. Add 1–2 tablespoons water and steam-cook the asparagus until just tender.

Lift the fish and mushrooms from the cooking liquid and place onto a dish. Strain the cooking liquid into a small saucepan and boil down by at least half. Add the cream, return to the boil and simmer until creamy. Whisk remaining butter into the sauce.

Place three asparagus spears on each plate. Top with a fish fillet and coat the fish with the delicious champagne sauce.

Garnish with tarragon leaves and serve.

SERVES 2

SÉTOISE FISH STEW

Bourride Sétoise
From the Languedoc-Roussillon Region
by Alain Gegnani

⸙————ᴕᴕᴕ————⸙

1 teaspoon dijon mustard
1 egg
1 egg yolk
1 teaspoon red wine vinegar
100 ml (3½ fl oz) extra virgin
olive oil
6 silverbeet leaves,
without the stalk
1 small leek, white part only,
cut into pieces
1 small celery stalk,
cut into pieces
1 carrot, cut into pieces
2 tablespoons extra olive oil
1 kg (2 lb 3 oz) monkfish tail,
cut into 16 pieces
85 ml (3 fl oz/⅓ cup) Noilly Prat
(vermouth)
salt
freshly ground pepper
a pinch of cayenne pepper
a pinch of saffron
3 cloves garlic, finely chopped
8 slices of baguette,
10 cm (3½ in) long × 2 cm (⅔ in)
thick, toasted

This local speciality of the picturesque seaside town of Sète, which borders the Mediterranean Sea, is popular because it's so tasty but also because the French love the texture and flavour of monkfish.

In a small blender, place the mustard, whole egg, egg yolk and vinegar and blend for 10 seconds. Bit by bit, add the olive oil, blending until thick. This is a type of mayonnaise. Transfer the mayonnaise to a bowl.

Place the silverbeet leaves, leek, celery and carrot in the blender and mix until well chopped but not quite puréed.

Heat the extra 2 tablespoons of olive oil in a frying pan. Add the chopped vegetables and stir for a few seconds. Add the monkfish pieces and stir on medium heat for a few seconds. Add the Noilly Prat and season with salt, pepper, cayenne pepper and saffron. Bring to the boil, cover and cook for about 8–10 minutes, turning the fish every minute or so.

Transfer the fish pieces onto four warm plates. Turn off the heat under the pan and slowly stir in two-thirds of the garlic and the mayonnaise to thicken the sauce.

Spoon the sauce over the fish and serve with the toasted bread brushed with the remaining garlic.

It's lovely served with steamed potatoes.

SERVES 4

MACKEREL
THE FLEMISH WAY

Maquereau à la Flamande
From the Northern France Region

100 g (3½ oz) butter, at room temperature
2 tablespoons finely chopped parsley
1 tablespoon finely chopped dill
1 shallot, finely chopped
1 tablespoon finely snipped chives
juice of ½ lemon
salt
freshly ground pepper
a pinch of nutmeg
2 fresh mackerels, cleaned and gutted
2 lemon wedges

The north of France benefits from the cold waters of the Channel, where some of the finest and tastiest fish are caught. Mackerel is a popular family meal as it's usually inexpensive and filling.

In a bowl mix 80 g (3 oz) of the butter with the parsley, dill, shallot, chives, lemon juice, a little salt and pepper and a pinch of nutmeg.

Fill the two mackerels with this herb butter. Place each mackerel on a piece of baking paper large enough to wrap the fish in. Brush the fish on both sides with the remaining butter (melted) and season with salt and pepper.

Wrap each fish in the baking paper and tie the parcels with kitchen string at each end and in the middle.

Place the fish on a hot grill plate or the flat plate of a barbecue and cook for about 10 minutes, turning the fish once, until it is cooked.

Carefully unwrap the fish and transfer onto plates. Spoon the hot melted herb butter over the fish and serve garnished with a lemon wedge.

SERVES 2

PAN-FRIED SALMON WITH SHALLOTS

Saumon poêlé aux échalottes
From the Pyrénées Region
by Philippe Mouchel

3 shallots, finely chopped
3 tablespoons sherry vinegar
4 tablespoons dry white wine
salt
freshly ground pepper
2 salmon fillets, skin on
1 tablespoon extra virgin olive oil
1 tablespoon butter
1 tablespoon finely chopped
tarragon leaves
chives

I first visited the Pyrénées region only a few years ago. It's a beautiful area of France with stunning mountains and valleys, lively markets and rustic, flavoursome food.

Place the shallots in a saucepan with the sherry vinegar and dry white wine and season with salt and pepper. Bring to a simmer and cook until almost all the liquid has evaporated.

Season the salmon fillets with salt and pepper.

Heat the olive oil in a non-stick pan and cook the fish, skin-side down, for about 5 minutes. Turn the fish over and remove the pan from the heat.

Return the shallot reduction to the heat, add the butter and tarragon and stir until the butter has melted.

Spread some of the shallot sauce on each plate. Top with the salmon, skin-side down, and spread a bit more sauce on top. Garnish with chives.

It's lovely served with steamed potatoes.

SERVES 2

SCAMPI & ARTICHOKE CRÊPES

*Crêpes aux langoustines
et aux artichauts*
From the Brittany Region

150 g (5 oz/1 cup) plain
(all-purpose) flour
salt
freshly ground pepper
1 egg
250 ml (8½ fl oz/1 cup) milk
80 g (3 oz) butter
2 tablespoons finely snipped chives
1 egg yolk mixed with 1 tablespoon
water
juice of ¼ lemon
2 tablespoons whipped cream
½ cup (60 g/ 2 oz) cooked
cauliflower florets
1 cup (220 g/7½ oz) cooked
artichoke hearts, cut into small
pieces
12 cooked scampi (10 peeled)

*The charming region of Brittany is known for its
delicious seafood. The Bretons love their crêpes and
this dish is a superb example of the regional taste.*

Place the flour, salt and pepper in a bowl. Make a well in the
centre and pour the egg and half the milk into the well. Whisk
the egg and milk together, then gradually incorporate the
flour, slowly adding the rest of the milk to form a smooth, thin
mixture. Rest this batter for 15 minutes.

Melt a teaspoon of butter in a crêpe pan. When it begins to
foam, whisk the melted butter into the crêpe batter. Stir in half
the chives as well.

Ladle enough crêpe batter into the pan to lightly coat the base.
Cook the first side then turn the crêpe to cook the other side.
Cook three more crêpes in the same way.

Place the egg yolk and water in a small bowl resting over a pan
of simmering water. Beat the yolk and water until it becomes
light and fluffy, then remove from heat.

Melt half the remaining butter, without boiling it, and then
bit by bit whisk it into the egg yolk in the bowl. Season with
lemon juice and fold in the whipped cream. This is called a
mousseline sauce.

Reheat the cauliflower, artichokes and scampi in the remaining
butter. Add the remaining chives.

On each crêpe, place two or three scampi tails and some
vegetables. Top with a little sauce and fold each crêpe.

Serve two crêpes per person, garnished with one
un-shelled scampi.

SERVES 2

YABBY TURNOVERS WITH TRUFFLE

Chausson d'écrevisses aux truffes
From the Alps Region

1 carrot
1 celery stalk, 20 cm (7 in) long
3 large mushrooms
2 tablespoons butter
½ tablespoon red wine vinegar
salt
freshly ground pepper
8–12 shelled and cleaned yabbies,
depending on size
4 rounds of rolled puff pastry,
about 12 cm (4 in) diameter x 3
mm (⅛ in) thick
1 egg yolk mixed with
1 teaspoon water
10 g (⅓ oz) fresh truffle, cut into
fine sticks

Yabbies are a much-loved delicacy in France, especially in the Alps region, where they are found in its many streams and lakes. Prawns could also be used in this recipe.

Preheat the oven to 200°C (390°F/Gas 6).

Cut the carrot, celery and mushrooms into batons about 4 cm (1½ in) long x 2 mm (1⁄13 in) thick.

Heat the butter in a frying pan. Add the vinegar and bring to the boil. Add the vegetables and stir-fry until they are soft but still a bit crunchy, then remove from the heat. Season the vegetables with salt and pepper, then briefly stir in the yabbies. Allow to cool.

Lay the puff pastry rounds on the bench and brush the edges with a little diluted egg yolk.

In the centre of each pastry round, place 1 tablespoon of vegetables, two or three yabbies and a little of the fresh truffle. Fold the pastry rounds over, into the shape of a turnover, and seal the edges by pressing with a fork. Brush the top with the remaining diluted egg yolk and make a light criss-cross pattern on top with a fork.

Bake the turnovers in the preheated oven for about 20 minutes until the pastry is well cooked.

SERVES 4

POULTRY
& RABBIT

CHICKEN CASSEROLE VALLÉE D'AUGE

Poulet Vallée d'Auge
From the Normandy Region

90 g (3 oz) butter
8 chicken pieces, on the bone, skin on
20 ml (⅔ fl oz) calvados liqueur
salt
freshly ground pepper
3 shallots, cut into quarters
150 ml (5 fl oz) cider
250 g (8½ oz) mushrooms
2 apples
210 ml (7½ fl oz/¾ cup) cream

The popularity of this dish doesn't surprise me. The sweetness of the cooked apples and creamy sauce is a real winner, and it is an easy-to-prepare dish for a special occasion.

Heat one-third of the butter in a large cast-iron pan and brown the chicken pieces on all sides. Then pour in the calvados. Season with salt and pepper. Add the shallots and cider and shake the pan. Bring to a simmer and then cover with foil and a lid and cook on low heat for 30 minutes.

Meanwhile, heat another third of the butter in a separate frying pan and cook the mushrooms for a few minutes.

Peel, halve and core the apples. Cut each half into four segments.

Heat the remaining butter in a large pan and cook the apple segments until soft.

Add the mushrooms to the chicken, then add the cream and mix well. Bring to a simmer and cook for about 5 minutes.

Serve the chicken and sauce on a large platter surrounded by the apple pieces.

SERVES 4

CHICKEN FRICASSEE WITH CHESTNUTS

Fricassée de poulet aux marrons
From the Rhône Valley Region
by Philippe Mouchel

1 chicken, cut into pieces, skin on
salt
freshly ground pepper
4 tablespoons extra virgin olive oil
3 tablespoons butter
2 cloves garlic, whole
4 sprigs of thyme
1 bay leaf
3 celery stalks, cut into sticks
about 5 cm (2 in) long x
1 cm (⅓ in) wide
250 g (8½ oz) peeled chestnuts
150 ml (5 fl oz) rich chicken stock
a few celery leaves

The French love the unique texture and flavour of chestnuts, and chicken with chestnuts is a great French classic. During my youth in France, we often collected large quantities of chestnuts from the local forest.

Preheat the oven to 170°C (340°F/Gas 3).

Season the chicken pieces with salt and pepper.

Heat 2 tablespoons olive oil in an ovenproof saucepan. Add 1 tablespoon butter and brown the chicken pieces on all sides. Stir in the garlic cloves and add the herbs. Bake in the preheated oven for about 10 minutes.

Transfer the chicken to a plate and keep warm. Discard the herbs and remove the excess fat from the pan.

Add the celery sticks, peeled chestnuts and 1 tablespoon butter and stir well for 2 minutes.

Return the chicken pieces to the pan, add the stock and return the pan to the oven to bake for 10 minutes.

Transfer the chicken to serving plates.

Add the remaining butter and 1 tablespoon olive oil to the cooking juices and vegetables in the pan and boil down for about 2 minutes to reduce the sauce.

Serve the chestnuts, celery and sauce around the chicken. Garnish with celery leaves and drizzle the remaining olive oil over the top.

SERVES 4

CHICKEN MARENGO WITH OLIVES

Poulet Marengo aux olives
From the Corsica Region

4 tablespoons extra virgin olive oil

8 chicken pieces, on the bone, skin on

3 tablespoons finely chopped shallots

2 tablespoons finely chopped lemon thyme

4 thin strips of orange zest

100 ml (3½ fl oz) dry white wine

500 g (1 lb 2 oz/2 cups) peeled, diced tomatoes

30 olives

salt

freshly ground pepper

20 broad beans (fava), shelled, blanched and skin removed

2 tablespoons chopped parsley

Napoleon Bonaparte's cook created this dish for the emperor after the Battle of Marengo in northern Italy. Bonaparte won the battle and enjoyed this Franco-Italian-style meal. It's delicious served with delicate broad beans.

Preheat the oven to 160°C (320°F/Gas 2).

Heat half the olive oil in a frying pan and brown the chicken pieces, skin-side down, for a few minutes. Transfer the chicken to a roasting tray and finish cooking in the preheated oven for about 15 minutes.

Remove the chicken fat from the roasting tray. Add the remaining oil, shallots, thyme and orange zest and stir for a few minutes. Stir in the wine and bring to the boil. Add the tomatoes, stir well and cook for 10 minutes.

Add the chicken pieces and olives to the sauce, season with salt and pepper, and heat through on low heat.

Serve the chicken and the sauce with broad beans, sprinkled with chopped parsley.

SERVES 8

GRANDMÈRE'S CHICKEN CASSEROLE

Poulet cocotte grandmère
From the Bresse Region

2 tablespoons butter
3 tablespoons vegetable oil
4 free-range chicken drumsticks, skin on
4 free-range chicken thighs, skin on
salt
freshly ground pepper
1 brown onion, diced
1 bay leaf
2 tablespoons rosemary sprigs
150 g (5 oz) bacon, diced
125 ml (4½ fl oz/½ cup) white Macon wine or another dry white wine
2 cups (180 g/6½ oz) button mushrooms, washed
4 medium all-purpose potatoes, cubed
3 tablespoons chopped parsley

The region of Bresse is famous for producing some of the tastiest chicken in France and this easy, delicious local recipe is one of our children's favourite dishes.

Heat the butter and 1 tablespoon of the oil in a wide heavy frying pan and brown the chicken pieces for a few minutes. Season with salt and pepper, add the onion, bay leaf and rosemary and stir well. Add the bacon and cook for a few minutes.

Add the white wine and bring to the boil. Stir in the mushrooms then cover with foil and a lid. Cook on low heat for about 30 minutes.

Heat the remaining oil in a heavy frying pan and cook the potato cubes for about 15 minutes or until they are almost done. Transfer the potatoes to the chicken dish and mix gently. Cook for a further 5 minutes to combine the flavours.

Serve two pieces of chicken on each plate with the vegetables. Garnish with parsley.

SERVES 4

DUCK LEG WITH PRUNES

Cuisse de canard rôtie aux pruneaux
From the Pyrénées/South West Region

2 duck legs, skin on
1 tablespoon extra virgin olive oil
sea salt
½ teaspoon cracked pepper
½ teaspoon fennel seeds, crushed
1 large carrot, peeled and sliced
2 tablespoons butter
1 shallot, finely chopped
2 tablespoons red wine
4 tablespoons rich chicken stock
10 prunes

The production of duck liver paté is big in the South West and duck meat is plentiful. It is common family fare prepared in many different ways. This easy recipe is ideal for a special occasion.

Preheat the oven to 180°C (350°F/Gas 4).

Rub the duck legs with olive oil and season the skin with salt, pepper and crushed fennel seeds.

Place the duck legs in a small roasting tray and bake in the preheated oven, skin-side up, for about 30 minutes, basting from time to time.

Meanwhile, steam the carrot in a little water until cooked. Drain the carrot, blend to a purée, stir in half the butter and season to taste.

Transfer the duck to a plate and cover with foil. Drain the duck fat from the tray, then add the shallots and cook for a few minutes. Add the red wine, stir and bring to the boil, evaporate most of it. Add the stock and bring to a simmer, then add the prunes and simmer for a further few minutes.

Stir in the remaining butter. Add the duck legs to the sauce and coat them.

Place a little carrot purée on each plate. Top with the duck, spoon the sauce and prunes on top and serve.

SERVES 2

1817

DUCK WITH TURNIPS

Canard aux navets
From the Pyrénées Region

2 turnips
125 ml (4 ½ fl oz/½ cup) water
1 tablespoon butter
2 duck breast fillets, skin on
1 teaspoon fennel seeds
salt
freshly ground pepper
1 shallot, finely chopped
1 tablespoon cognac
2 tablespoons veal glaze
2 tablespoons extra water

Many years ago, duck was only available whole and it was mostly eaten at restaurants, but now it is easy to buy in a variety of cuts and duck has become a common and much-loved family treat.

Peel the turnips and cut each into six segments. Using a paring knife, trim the turnips into large olive shapes, the size of a date.

Place the turnips, the water and half the butter in a saucepan and cook on medium heat until the turnips are soft and the water has evaporated. By that time, the turnips will be glazed by the butter.

Meanwhile, season the skin of the duck fillets with fennel seeds and a little salt and pepper.

Heat a heavy frying pan. Place the duck, skin-side down, in the hot pan and cook on medium heat for about 8 minutes. Turn the duck over and cook for a further 2 minutes. Transfer the duck fillets to a warm plate and cover with foil.

Discard the duck fat from the pan. Put the shallots into the pan and cook for 2 minutes.

Add the cognac and flame it before adding the veal glaze and 2 tablespoons water. Simmer for 1 minute, then stir in the remaining butter.

Reheat the turnips in the sauce.

Cut each duck fillet into three pieces and serve on warm plates with the turnips and sauce.

SERVES 2

ROAST GUINEA FOWL WITH SPINACH & PEARS

*Pintade rôtie aux épinards
et aux poires*
From the Pyrénées Region

3 sprigs of rosemary, about 10 cm (3½ in) long
4–5 cloves garlic, whole
1 guinea fowl, about 1 kg (2 lb 3 oz)
salt
freshly ground pepper
1 tablespoon extra virgin olive oil
30 g (1 oz) butter
½ brown onion, diced
½ cup (70 g/2½ oz) diced celery
2 just ripe pears (William pears are good)
2 cups (100g/3 oz) spinach leaves, washed
2 tablespoons pouring cream
2 tablespoons dry white wine
75 ml (2½ fl oz/¼ cup) cold water
2 finely chopped mint leaves

I'm always a bit surprised that outside France few restaurants serve guinea fowl. In France it's a popular Sunday lunch treat and this recipe is delicious.

Preheat the oven to 160°C (320°F/Gas 2).

Place the rosemary and garlic cloves in the cavity of the guinea fowl and season the bird with salt and pepper.

Heat the oil and 10 g (⅓ oz) butter in a flameproof baking pan and brown the guinea fowl on each side for 1–2 minutes. Place the onion and celery around the bird, then roast it in the preheated oven for about 45 minutes, basting once or twice during the cooking.

Meanwhile, peel, halve and core the pears. Cut each half into four segments.

Heat 10 g (⅓ oz) butter in a wide frying pan and cook the pears for a few minutes on each side.

Cook the spinach in a saucepan of boiling water until wilted. Drain the spinach and press by hand to extract the excess water.

Add the cream to the pears, stir in the spinach and reheat.

Remove the guinea fowl from the baking pan and keep warm.

Add the wine to the baking pan and bring to a simmer. Add the water and boil for about 2 minutes. Strain the juices into a small saucepan and stir in the remaining butter and the mint leaves.

Portion the guinea fowl into eight pieces. Put some spinach and pear onto each plate and top with three or four pieces of guinea fowl. Spoon a little sauce over the top and serve.

SERVES 2

WILD RABBIT STEW COOKED IN GAILLAC WINE

Civet de lapin au vin de Gaillac
From the South West Region

1 wild rabbit, cut into portions
1 carrot, sliced
1 cup (125 g/4½ oz) sliced celery
about 10 parsley sprigs
2 sprigs of thyme
1 bay leaf
2 shallots, sliced
1 teaspoon cracked pepper
½ bottle red Gaillac wine or
another full-bodied red wine
½ cup (75 g/2½ oz) diced bacon
2 tablespoons plain
(all-purpose) flour
salt
2 cups (180 g/6½ oz) quartered
mushrooms
1 tablespoon butter
2–3 tablespoons chopped parsley

The scenery of the Tarn valley around the town of Albi in the South West is quite superb. The local food is rustic and the Gaillac wines are strong and fruity, complementing the gamey flavour of this dish.

Place the rabbit pieces in a wide bowl with the carrots, celery, parsley, thyme, bay leaf, shallot and cracked pepper. Add the red wine, stir briefly, cover with plastic wrap and marinate overnight in the fridge.

The next day, preheat the oven to 140°C (280°F/Gas 1). Drain the rabbit pieces and strain the red wine marinade into a bowl, reserving the vegetables and herbs.

Stir-fry the bacon in a non-stick frying pan for 1 minute and then transfer to a plate.

Place the rabbit pieces in the non-stick pan and cook, stirring for a few minutes. Add the flour and stir for 2–3 minutes. Stir in the marinade liquid and bring to a simmer. Pour the vegetables and herbs over the rabbit. Season with salt, cover with foil and a lid and cook in the preheated oven for about 2 hours.

A little before serving, cook the mushrooms in butter for a few minutes, then add the mushrooms and bacon to the rabbit. Reheat for a few minutes. Spoon some of the rabbit stew onto each plate and garnish with chopped parsley.

This is delicious served with boiled potatoes.

SERVES 3

HARE & RED WINE STEW

Civet de lièvre au vin d'Arbois
From the Franche-Comté Region

1 hare, about 1 kg (2 lb 3 oz), cut into portions (2 front legs, 2 back legs and the body cut into 4 pieces)

1 brown onion, sliced

1 medium carrot, sliced

3 cloves garlic, crushed

1 bay leaf

2 cloves

3 sprigs of thyme

2 tablespoons brandy

625 ml (22 fl oz/2½ cups) red Arbois wine or another medium-bodied red wine

2 tablespoons vegetable oil

1 tablespoon butter

salt

freshly ground pepper

1½ tablespoons plain (all-purpose) flour

3 tablespoons chopped parsley

I have always liked the richness of hare meat. When I was a boy, my grandmother often cooked hare during the winter hunting season. Hare can be ordered from a good poultry shop.

Place the hare pieces in a bowl with the onion, carrot, crushed garlic, bay leaf, cloves, thyme, brandy and red wine. Cover the bowl with plastic wrap, refrigerate and leave to marinate overnight.

The next day, preheat the oven to 140°C (280°F/Gas 1).

Drain the hare pieces on kitchen paper. Strain the liquid into a bowl, reserving the vegetables and herbs.

Heat the oil and butter on medium heat in a flameproof casserole dish and brown the hare pieces on all sides. Season with salt and pepper and stir in the vegetables and herbs, cook for a few minutes. Dust with flour and stir well. Stir in the marinade liquid and bring to a simmer. Cover with foil and a lid and bake in the preheated oven for about 2½ hours.

Transfer the cooked hare pieces to a platter. Strain the rich sauce over the meat, discarding the vegetables and herbs. Sprinkle the meat with chopped parsley.

I love it served with pasta such as pappardelle.

SERVES 4-5

BEEF, LAMB
& PORK

BEEF CHEEK STEW IN MADIRAN WINE

Estoufat de joue de boeuf au Madiran
From the Midi-Pyrénées Region

½ brown onion, diced

2 rashers of bacon, diced

3 cloves garlic, sliced

1 medium carrot, sliced

salt

freshly ground pepper

2 cloves, sliced

a pinch of cinnamon

a pinch of grated nutmeg

1 very thin slice of pork fat, about 15 cm (6 in) square (alternatively, use slices of bacon fat)

3 beef cheeks, trimmed

bouquet garni, made up of 6 sprigs of parsley, 2 sprigs of thyme and 1 bay leaf, tied together with kitchen string

125 ml (4 ½ fl oz/½ cup) Madiran red wine or another full-bodied red wine

125 ml (4 ½ fl oz/½ cup) rich beef stock or broth

3 tablespoons chopped parsley

One of the great characteristics of French cuisine is the use of red wine in meat dishes. The wine tenderises the meat and adds rich flavour to the gravy of delicious slow-cooked cuts, like beef cheek.

Preheat the oven to 140°C (280°F/Gas 1).

In a bowl, mix together the onion, bacon, garlic, carrot, salt, pepper, cloves, cinnamon and nutmeg.

Line the base of a medium casserole dish with the pork fat. Top with half of the vegetable mix, then cover with the beef cheeks. Add the bouquet garni, then sprinkle the remaining vegetables on top. Add the wine and beef stock, and cover with foil and a lid.

Bake in the preheated oven for about 3 hours or until the beef is very tender.

Place a beef cheek onto each plate and spoon over the sauce and vegetables, then garnish with chopped parsley.

It is delicious served with mashed potato.

SERVES 3

POACHED BEEF WITH SPRING VEGETABLES

*Boeuf à la ficelle aux
légumes du printemps*
From the Paris/Ile de France Region

1 litre (34 fl oz/4 cups) rich beef
broth or stock, well seasoned with
salt and pepper
12 baby carrots, peeled
8 bite-size pieces of celery
3 broad beans (fava), shelled
2 x 180 g (6 oz) pieces of beef eye
fillet from the middle
1 tablespoon finely chopped herbs;
e.g. parsley, dill or chervil

*This wonderful classic French dish of tender eye fillet
poached slowly in a rich broth is served with the
sweetest spring vegetables.*

Bring the rich broth to a simmer in a small saucepan. Add the
carrots and celery pieces and the shelled broad beans to the
broth, cook for 1 minute, then remove the broad beans using a
slotted spoon. Cool the broad beans in cold water, peel them
and place in another small saucepan.

When the carrots and celery are cooked, transfer them to the
broad beans, with a little of the beef broth.

Tie neatly each slice of beef with two rounds of kitchen string.
Place the meat in the simmering rich stock and poach for
5–8 minutes, depending on how cooked you like your meat to
be. When cooked, transfer the meat to a plate and remove
the string.

Serve this dish in deep plates. Arrange the warm vegetables in
each plate plus about 4 tablespoons of broth.

Cut each piece of meat in half and place in the centre of the
vegetables. Garnish the vegetables with fresh herbs.

It is lovely served with salt, pepper and mustard.

SERVES 2

BEEF SHIN STEWED WITH CARROTS

Jarret de boeuf aux carottes
From the Limousin Region

⸻⸻⸻

2 tablespoons extra virgin olive oil
1 shin of beef with the bone, trimmed of fat
½ brown onion, diced
2 rashers of bacon, diced
1 medium carrot, diced
½ cup (70 g/2½ oz) diced celery
3 cloves garlic, crushed
1 clove
1 tablespoon plain (all-purpose) flour
1 tablespoon tomato paste (concentrated purée)
250 ml (8½ cup fl oz/1 cup) rich beef stock
100 ml (3½ fl oz) dry white wine
bouquet garni, made up of a few sprigs of parsley, thyme and a bay leaf tied together with kitchen string
salt
freshly ground pepper
8 medium carrots, peeled
chopped parsley

The Limousin region in central France is famous for its breed of cattle, which produces some of the tastiest beef in France. Share this wonderful winter classic with good friends over a bottle of your best red.

Preheat the oven to 120°C (250°F/Gas ½).

Heat the olive oil in a large, non-stick frying pan and brown the beef shin for a few minutes. Transfer the shin to a large, cast-iron pan.

Add the onion and bacon to the non-stick pan and stir for 1 minute. Add the diced carrot and celery, the garlic and clove and stir for a couple of minutes. Stir in the flour and tomato paste, then add the beef stock, wine and the bouquet garni. Season with salt and pepper. Bring to the boil and stir well.

Transfer to the cast-iron pan with the meat. Cover the pan with foil and a lid and cook in the preheated oven for about 3 hours, turning the meat over once or twice.

Add the eight carrots and stir briefly. Cover the pan again and finish cooking in the oven for a further hour or so.

Transfer the beef, carrots and sauce to a warm platter and garnish with chopped parsley ready to serve.

SERVES 4-6

VEAL & MUSHROOM SAUTÉ WITH RÔSTI

Veau sauté aux champignons et rösti
From the Alps and Swiss Region

2 medium all-purpose potatoes,
boiled in their skins
1 brown onion, chopped
salt
freshly ground pepper
2 tablespoons vegetable oil
60 g (2 oz) butter
450 g (1 lb) veal tenderloin, well
trimmed and finely sliced
250 g (9 oz) Swiss brown
mushrooms, sliced
50 ml (2 fl oz) dry white wine
125 ml (4 ½ fl oz/½ cup) pouring
cream
3 tablespoons chopped parsley

Veal is an extremely popular meat in the Alps, especially Switzerland and in France along the Swiss border. This recipe is popular all over the world and is sure to please.

Peel and grate the potatoes. Mix them in a bowl with half the onion and season with salt and pepper.

In a medium non-stick frying pan, heat half the oil and half the butter. Place three mounds of grated potato in the pan, pressing them down to form three rösti (in the shape of a burger), each about 1 cm (⅓ in) thick. Cook for several minutes then very gently turn them over and cook the other side. Put aside and keep warm.

Heat the remaining oil and butter in a large non-stick pan and brown the veal on high heat for a short time. Transfer the veal to a plate.

Add the remaining chopped onion to the pan and stir for 1 minute. Add the mushrooms and cook for a few minutes. Add the white wine, bring to the boil and evaporate the wine a little. Stir in the cream, bring to the boil and boil for 1 minute. Season well with salt and pepper.

Add the veal to the pan and reheat briefly.

Place a rösti in the centre of each plate and arrange the veal and the mushroom sauce around it. Sprinkle with parsley and serve.

SERVES 3

VEAL CUTLETS WITH MUSHROOMS & COMTÉ

Côtes de veau panés aux champignons et Comté
From the French Jura Region
by Philippe Mouchel

3 veal cutlets
salt
freshly ground pepper
6 slices of prosciutto-style ham
6 slices of Swiss-style cheese
plain (all-purpose) flour
1 egg, beaten
½ cup (50 g/2 oz) fine dried breadcrumbs
2 tablespoons extra virgin olive oil
3 tablespoons butter
3 sprigs of thyme
5 cloves garlic (2 whole, 2 crushed, 1 chopped)
3 cups (270 g/9 oz) mixed mushrooms, chopped
1 shallot, chopped
3 tablespoons chopped parsley
juice of ½ lemon

The huge Comté cheese from the Jura region is so delicious that it's one of the three or four most popular cheeses in France. It's also a superb cooking cheese and is wonderful in this veal dish.

Make a horizontal cut through the centre of the veal cutlets, from the edge to the bone. Butterfly and season the cutlets with salt and pepper.

On one side of each cutlet, place a thin slice of ham, then two slices of cheese and lastly another slice of ham, then fold the meat on top like a sandwich and press together.

Set up three plates, one with flour, one with beaten egg and one with breadcrumbs. Dust each cutlet with a little plain flour, then dip each side in the beaten egg. Lastly, coat each cutlet with a thin layer of breadcrumbs.

Heat 1 tablespoon olive oil and 1 tablespoon butter in a frying pan. Add the thyme, 2 whole cloves of garlic and the veal and cook the cutlets on each side for 5 minutes.

Heat 1 tablespoon olive oil and 1 tablespoon butter in a second frying pan. Add 2 crushed cloves of garlic and the mushrooms, season with a little salt and pepper and cook for a few minutes on medium heat. Add the chopped shallot, the remaining clove of chopped garlic and some of the parsley.

Spoon the mushrooms onto each plate and top with a veal cutlet.

Melt the remaining butter in a pan, then add the lemon juice and remaining parsley. Spoon the sauce over the meat and serve.

SERVES 3

LAMB STEW WITH SPRING VEGETABLES

Navarin d'agneau printanier
From the Pyrénées Region
by Philippe Mouchel

2 tablespoons extra virgin olive oil

1 tablespoon butter

1 kg (2 lb 3 oz) deboned lamb shoulder or neck, cut into 15–20 pieces

1 medium carrot, diced

1 medium onion, diced

2 tablespoons plain (all-purpose) flour

3 ripe tomatoes, diced

750 ml (26 fl oz/3 cups) chicken stock

2 cloves garlic, chopped

bouquet garni, made up of a few sprigs of parsley, thyme and a bay leaf, tied together with kitchen string

salt

freshly ground pepper

8 baby carrots

8 small turnips

1½ cups (230 g/8 oz) shelled peas

8 small onions

8 baby potatoes

chopped parsley

I love to visit the stunning Pyrénées region at the end of spring when most of the snow has melted. The grass looks so rich that it's easy to understand why the local lamb is so good.

Preheat the oven to 150°C (300°F/Gas 2).

Heat the oil and butter in a flameproof casserole and brown the lamb pieces on all sides for a few minutes. Add the diced carrot and onion and stir for 2 minutes. Stir in the flour to coat the meat well, then add the tomatoes and stir for 1 minute. Add the stock, garlic and bouquet garni. Mix well and season with salt and pepper.

Cover with a lid and cook in the preheated oven for about 2 hours.

Meanwhile, steam the baby carrots, turnips, peas, small onions and potatoes in a saucepan.

Add the vegetables to the tender meat, stir well and reheat.

Serve sprinkled with chopped parsley.

SERVES 4

LAMB SHANKS WITH THYME & OLIVES

*Jarret d'agneau au thym
et aux olives*
From the Northern Provence Region

⊰————⟆

4 lamb shanks

salt

freshly ground pepper

4 sprigs of lemon thyme, finely
chopped

3 tablespoons extra virgin olive oil

1 brown onion, diced

3 cloves garlic, crushed

2 medium fennel bulbs, each cut
into 8 segments

1 green capsicum (pepper), cut
into bite-size pieces

1 red capsicum (pepper), cut into
bite-size pieces

3 medium tomatoes, quartered

75 ml (2½ fl oz) dry white wine

30 baby olives

*Northern Provence is one of my favourite regions in
my homeland. Just thinking of it evokes aromas of its
colourful cuisine packed with fresh herbs and tasty
vegetables.*

Preheat the oven to 140°C (280°F/Gas 1).

Season the lamb shanks with salt, pepper and the finely
chopped lemon thyme.

Heat the olive oil in an ovenproof pan and brown the meat for a
few minutes.

Add the onion and garlic and stir briefly. Add the fennel,
capsicum (pepper) and tomatoes, making sure to distribute
the vegetables evenly in the pan. Add the wine and bring to a
simmer.

Cover the pan with a lid and cook in the preheated oven for
about 2 hours until the meat is tender. During the cooking stir
the vegetables and turn the meat a couple of times.

Transfer the cooked meat and vegetables to a dish.

Boil down the pan juices to a sauce consistency. Add the
olives and stir for 10 seconds.

Spoon some of the vegetables onto each plate. Top with a
lamb shank and spoon the sauce and olives over the top.

SERVES 4

LAMB & BEAN STEW

Pistache de mouton
From the Pyrénées Region

1 tablespoon butter
50 g (2 oz) fatty bacon, diced
3 sprigs of thyme, chopped
12 pieces of lamb from the shoulder, each about 80 g (3 oz)
1 small onion, diced
4 cloves garlic, crushed
1 bay leaf
salt
freshly ground pepper
75 ml (2½ fl oz/¼ cup) dry white wine
2 tomatoes, diced
400 g (14 oz) cooked white beans, drained
4 tablespoons chopped parsley
6 tablespoons dried breadcrumbs

The mountain range between France and Spain is called the Pyrénées, and the cuisine of this region is very hearty, perfect for the cold weather in the mountains. This delicious local dish takes a few hours to cook but is easy to prepare and really worth it.

Heat the butter and bacon in a wide heavy saucepan. Add the thyme and stir well. Add the lamb pieces and brown the lamb on all sides for a few minutes.

Add the onion, garlic and bay leaf and season with salt and pepper. Cook for 4–5 minutes to lightly brown the onion.

Add the wine, bring to the boil, then add the tomatoes. Cover with foil and the lid and cook on low heat for about 1½–2 hours until the meat is tender. Stir the stew a couple of times during the cooking to make sure it doesn't stick.

When the meat is cooked, add the beans. Stir gently and reheat for a few minutes. Transfer the stew to a wide gratin dish and sprinkle the top with the chopped parsley and breadcrumbs.

Place under a hot grill and leave for a few minutes until golden brown. Serve immediately but take care as it is very hot.

SERVES 4-6

LOIN OF LAMB WITH BROAD BEANS & FINE HERBS

Noisettes d'agneau aux fèves
et aux fines herbes
From the Aquitaine/Bordeaux Region

2 x 150 g (5 oz) loins of lamb,
trimmed of fat and skin

1 clove garlic, finely sliced

3–4 sprigs of lemon thyme,
chopped

freshly ground pepper

1½ tablespoons extra
virgin olive oil

6 baby carrots, peeled

3 tablespoons water

1 cup (175 g/6 oz) shelled broad
beans (fava)

salt

75 ml (2½ fl oz/¼ cup) dry white
wine

½ tablespoon butter

about 10 tarragon leaves

fresh herbs (mint leaves and
chervil)

The lamb from Paulliac in the Bordeaux region is known as some of the best in France. Open a bottle of your finest red wine to enjoy with this lovely dinner-party dish.

Cut each loin of lamb into five pieces. In French the cut is called *noisette*. In a bowl, season the noisettes with the sliced garlic, chopped lemon thyme, a little pepper and 1 tablespoon olive oil. Combine and then put aside for 30 minutes.

Place the carrots in a small saucepan with ½ tablespoon olive oil and 3 tablespoons water and simmer, covered, for about 8 minutes.

Place the shelled broad beans in a saucepan of boiling water. Drain after 3 minutes. When cool enough to handle, peel the broad beans and put aside in a bowl.

Heat a non-stick frying pan and cook the lamb noisettes, seasoned with salt, for about 2–3 minutes on each side. Transfer the noisettes to a dish.

Add the dry white wine to the pan and bring to the boil. Add the carrots and their cooking juices, the broad beans, the butter and the tarragon leaves.

Arrange five pieces of lamb on each plate. Spoon the vegetables and cooking juices in between the noisettes, garnish with a few mint leaves and chervil leaves and serve.

SERVES 2

ROAST LAMB WITH FLAGEOLETS

Gigot d'agneau aux flageolets
From the Normandy Region

❦————✠————

12 cloves garlic
1 leg of spring lamb, trimmed of most of the fat
1 tablespoon extra virgin olive oil
3 tablespoons butter, softened
salt
freshly ground pepper
4 medium carrots, cut into 1½ cm (½ in) slices
75 ml (2½ fl oz/¼ cup) dry cider
2 cups (550 g/20 oz) drained cooked flageolet beans (alternatively, borlotti or haricot beans)
3 tablespoons chopped parsley

The sheep that graze on the coastal fields of Normandy eat a rich, salty grass that gives the lamb meat a superb flavour. A tradition in the region is to bake lamb at Easter, often served with baked beans. Flageolets are small, delicate beans, light-green in colour.

Preheat the oven to 180°C (350°F/Gas 4).

Peel four garlic cloves and cut each clove lengthways into four slivers.

Using the tip of a small knife blade, make 16 cuts into the lamb at regular intervals, ensuring the cuts are deep enough to hold the pieces of garlic. Push the slivers of garlic into the cuts.

Oil a roasting pan. Place the leg of lamb in the pan and rub it all over with half the butter. Season the lamb with salt and pepper and bake it in the preheated oven for about 45 minutes, turning it two or three times during the cooking so it cooks evenly.

After 20 minutes of cooking, add the carrot slices and remaining garlic cloves to the pan.

When the meat is done, remove it from the oven, transfer to a dish, cover with foil and leave to rest for about 10 minutes.

Remove the excess fat from the roasting pan, add the cider and bring to the boil. Add the flageolet beans and the remaining butter and heat. Stir in the chopped parsley.

Serve two or three tablespoons of beans and carrots on each plate and a few thin slices of lamb.

SERVES 8

ROAST RACK OF LAMB WITH SPRING VEGETABLES

Carré d'agneau rôti aux légumes printaniers
From the Paris Region

---

2 x 3-cutlet racks of lamb, trimmed of fat
2 tablespoons extra virgin olive oil
freshly ground pepper
1 tablespoon chopped rosemary leaves
1 cup (175 g/6 oz) shelled broad beans (fava)
4 baby carrots, peeled
½ cup (75 g/2½ oz) shelled peas
tips of 4 fat asparagus spears
1 tablespoon butter
8 tarragon leaves
salt

Paris is surrounded by large areas of farmland where vegetables are grown and then sold in the many superb markets dotted throughout the city. There are actually more than fifty open-air markets in Paris.

Preheat the oven to 150°C (300°F/Gas 2).

Brush the racks of lamb with a little olive oil and season with pepper and rosemary leaves.

Heat a small ovenproof pan and brown the lamb racks for 1 minute. Bake in the preheated oven for about 10 minutes.

Remove the pan from the oven, cover the meat with foil and rest for 10 minutes.

Meanwhile, drop the broad beans into a small saucepan of boiling water and cook for 1 minute. Lift the broad beans out of the water and refresh in a bowl of cold water.

Place the baby carrots in the boiling water and cook for 2 minutes. Add the peas to the boiling carrots, cook for 5 minutes, then add the asparagus. Cook the vegetables for a further 2 minutes, then drain and transfer them to a frying pan.

Add the peeled broad beans, the butter and tarragon leaves and season with a little salt and pepper and reheat briefly.

On each plate, place the rack of lamb, which can be carved before plating if you wish, over the spring vegetables. Spoon the tarragon-flavoured butter over the lamb and serve.

SERVES 2

ROAST SADDLE OF LAMB WITH HERBS

Selle d'agneau rôti aux herbes
From the Northern Provence Region

---

1 x 1.2 kg (2 lb 10 oz) deboned
saddle of lamb
4 tablespoons chopped parsley
2 tablespoons chopped tarragon
4 tablespoons chopped thyme
salt
freshly ground pepper
50 g (2 oz) butter, softened
3 tablespoons dried breadcrumbs
2 tablespoons extra virgin olive oil
3 different-coloured capsicums
(peppers), cut into bite-size pieces
6 cloves garlic, with the skin
a little extra olive oil

The lamb of northern Provence has a delicate meat that marries well with herbs. The saddle is a cut comprising the racks that are deboned but still held together by the skin. Ask your butcher to debone it for you.

Preheat the oven to 180°C (350°F/Gas 4).

Without damaging the skin, remove some of the excess fat from the top of the saddle.

Place the parsley, tarragon and thyme in a bowl. Season with salt and pepper and mix in the butter and breadcrumbs.

Place the deboned rack of lamb, skin-side down, on a board and spread the herb mixture over the meat. Roll the meat into a roast and tie it with about 10 rounds of kitchen string, 2 cm (⅔ in) apart.

Heat the olive oil in a small ovenproof pan and gently brown the roast on all sides. Place the capsicums (peppers) and garlic around the meat and roast in the preheated oven for 40 minutes.

Turn off the heat and rest the meat in the oven for about 10 minutes.

Cut the string and carve the meat into 3 cm (1 in) slices. Serve the meat with the capsicums and garlic, drizzle the meat with a little extra olive oil and pan juices.

SERVES 5-6

SLOW-COOKED SALTED PORK WITH LENTILS

Petit salé aux lentilles
From the Auvergne Region
by Philippe Mouchel

———

500 g (1 lb) pork belly
3 tablespoons sea salt
2 teaspoons cracked pepper
3 sprigs of thyme
1 onion, pierced with a clove
2 cloves garlic, whole
2 carrots
1 piece of leek, 10 cm (4 in) long
2 bouquet garni, each made up of a few sprigs parsley, thyme and a bay leaf, tied together with kitchen string
30 g (1 oz) pork fat
2 shallots, chopped
80 g (3 oz) bacon, diced
1½ cups (280 g/10 oz) lentils, boiled for 2 minutes then drained
750 ml (26 fl oz/3 cups) chicken stock
1 clove garlic extra, crushed
1 tablespoon butter
2 tablespoons chopped parsley

The central mountainous region of Auvergne is famous for its charcuterie and pork. This slow-cooked pork belly and lentil dish is popular with the locals and is often served in Parisian brasseries. You need to plan ahead when preparing this dish.

Place the pork belly on a plate and rub generously with sea salt. Season with cracked pepper and thyme, then cover in plastic wrap and refrigerate for at least 8 hours.

Remove the salted pork from the plastic wrap and place in a saucepan. Add the onion pierced with a clove, the whole garlic cloves, carrots, leek and 1 bouquet garni. Cover with water, bring to a simmer and simmer for 2–3 hours until tender.

Heat the pork fat in a saucepan. Add the shallots and stir for 1 minute. Add the bacon, stir well, then add the lentils. Cover with the chicken stock, add the extra garlic and remaining bouquet garni, and simmer until the lentils are soft, by which time the lentils will have absorbed almost all the stock. Stir in the butter.

Drain and slice the pork.

On each plate, place the lentils with a few carrots and some of the sliced pork. Sprinkle with parsley. If you wish, serve with mustard or drizzle a salad dressing with herbs over the dish.

SERVES 2-3

4 BOUCHERIE 4

CAKES &
SWEET
MORSELS

ALMOND & APRICOT CAKE

Gâteau aux amandes et aux abricots
From the Rhône-Alps Region

—◁—⋙—▷—

5 ripe apricots
150 g (5 oz) butter
100 g (3½ oz) caster sugar
3 eggs, at room temperature
75 ml (2½ fl oz/¼ cup) orange blossom honey
120 g (4 oz) ground almond
100 g (3½ oz) self-raising flour, sifted
1 tablespoon extra caster sugar
2 tablespoons flaked almonds
icing sugar for dusting

I urge you to try this cake when apricots are at their best. It's easy to make and I love it so much that I have planted an apricot tree in my garden!

Preheat the oven to 200°C (390°F/Gas 6). Butter and flour a 24 cm (9 in) cake tin.

Wash and halve the apricots and remove the stones.

Cream the butter and caster sugar for a few minutes until light and creamy, using an electric beater. Beat in the eggs and whisk in the honey. Then fold in the ground almond and flour.

Carefully pour the cake mixture into the prepared cake tin and tap the tin to distribute the mixture evenly. Arrange the apricot halves, cut-side up, attractively on top and sprinkle them with extra caster sugar. Sprinkle flaked almonds in the spaces between the apricots.

Bake the cake in the preheated oven for 45 minutes or until cooked.

Remove the cake from the oven and cool for 10 minutes before carefully turning out onto a wire rack. Allow to cool.

Dust the top with icing sugar just before serving.

SERVES 8

BORDEAUX CANELÉS

Canelés de Bordeaux
From the Bordeaux/Aquitaine Region
by Pierrick Boyer

1 litre (34 fl oz/4 cups) milk
1 vanilla pod, slit lengthways
60 g (2 oz) butter
620 g (1 lb 5 oz) caster sugar
310 g (11 oz) plain (all-purpose)
flour
1 egg, at room temperature
8 egg yolks, at room temperature
125 ml (4½ fl oz/½ cup) rum
200 g (7 oz) beeswax, melted

In France most people buy these little cakes at the pâtisserie, but experienced dessert makers will have fun making them. You will need special metal canelé moulds, and the cake mix needs to rest overnight in the fridge before being baked.

Pour three-quarters of the milk into a saucepan. Scrape the seeds of the vanilla pod into the milk and then add the vanilla pod. Heat the milk to almost boiling point. Add the butter to melt. Remove the pan from the heat and add the remaining cold milk.

Combine the caster sugar and flour in a bowl.

In another bowl, whisk the egg with the 8 egg yolks. Mix in the rum, the flour and sugar mixture and about a quarter of the warm milk, mixing until smooth. Little by little, add the remaining milk.

Refrigerate the preparation overnight. The next day, preheat the oven to 220°C (430°F/Gas 7).

Brush the canelé moulds lightly with melted beeswax. Fill the moulds with the mixture to about 5 mm (¼ in) below the rim. Place the filled moulds in the preheated oven and then reduce the oven to 180°C (350°F/Gas 4). Bake for about 45–50 minutes.

Carefully turn the canelés out onto a cake rack while still hot. Allow to cool.

MAKES ABOUT 50

BRIOCHE FROM VENDÉE

Brioche Vendéenne
From the Vendée Region
by Pierrick Boyer

---

500 g (1 lb 1 oz) plain (all-purpose)
flour
10 g (⅓ oz) salt
150 g (5 oz) caster sugar
15 g (½ oz) dry yeast
4 eggs, at room temperature
1 teaspoon orange flower water
300 g (10½ oz) butter
2 egg yolks mixed with
1 tablespoon water
3 tablespoons sesame seeds

As with many cakes, this special treat of Brioche Vendéenne is usually bought at the local pâtisserie or boulangerie by French families to serve to visitors. It's served with coffee and is often dunked in the coffee. Skilful home cooks will derive great pleasure from making brioche.

In the bowl of an electric beater, place the flour, salt, caster sugar, dry yeast, eggs and orange flower water and beat on medium speed until it forms a smooth, elastic dough.

Reduce to low speed, add the butter bit by bit and beat until well incorporated. This takes about 10 minutes.

Remove the dough from the bowl and form it into a long piece. Place it on a baking tray lined with baking paper, cover with a damp tea towel and leave to rise for 2 hours.

Flatten the dough into a long rectangle and cut it into three long pieces. Roll each piece into a long baguette shape and form a plait with the three pieces of dough. Place on another baking tray lined with baking paper and leave to prove for about 1 hour in a warm place.

Preheat the oven to 160°C (320°F/Gas 2).

Brush the risen dough lightly with the egg yolk mixture and sprinkle with sesame seeds. Bake in the preheated oven for about 30 minutes.

Cool the brioche before slicing.

SERVES 10-15

FRENCH TOASTED BRIOCHE

Brioche perdue
From the Beauce Region
(just south of Paris)

250 ml (8½ fl oz/1 cup) milk
3 tablespoons caster sugar
½ vanilla pod, slit lengthways
1 egg
1 piece of brioche loaf, about
12 cm (5 in) long
2 tablespoons butter
icing sugar for dusting
ground cinnamon for dusting

This easy-to-prepare French family classic was traditionally made using one-day-old bread but now it's often made with brioche as a breakfast treat. I serve it with red fruits, like raspberries.

Place the milk, half the caster sugar and the vanilla pod in a small saucepan. Bring to a simmer, then transfer to a wide dish to cool.

Beat the egg with the remaining caster sugar in a bowl.

Cut the brioche into six thick slices. Dip each slice in the cooled milk then lightly coat with the egg mix.

Heat the butter in a large frying pan and cook the brioche on each side until golden brown.

Generously dust the brioche with icing sugar and a little cinnamon. Serve immediately on its own or with red fruits.

SERVES 3

KOUIGN AMANN BRETON CAKE

Kouign Amann
From the Bretagne Region
by Jean-Marie Blanchot

—❦———————❧—

500 g (1 lb 1 oz) plain (all-purpose)
flour, sifted

1 teaspoon bread improver

320 ml (11 fl oz) cold water

15 g (½ oz) salt

10 g (⅓ oz) fresh compressed
yeast

350 g (12 oz) butter

300 g (10 oz) sugar

This Breton cake is a unique cross between a croissant and puff pastry. Few French people would make it at home, this recipe requires pastry skills – and patience!

Butter two cake tins, each about 24 cm (9½ in) in diameter.

In the bowl of an electric beater, place the flour, bread improver, water, salt and yeast and beat until it forms a dough. Shape the dough into a ball, cover with plastic film and refrigerate for about 1 hour.

On a floured bench, flatten the dough with a rolling pin to a square about 1 cm (⅓ in) thick and dust with flour.

Using the rolling pin, flatten the butter between two layers of baking paper to a 1 cm (⅓ in) thickness and place it in the centre of the dough. Fold the four edges of the dough into the middle to completely envelop the butter. Roll the pastry out to a rectangular strip about 1 cm (⅓ in) thick. Take the lower end of the strip and fold it up one-third of the way towards the top. Now fold the top down to fit over the first fold to form a neat rectangle with no overlapping sides.

Chill the dough for 30 minutes, then roll it out again to a long rectangle. Coat generously with sugar, then fold it into thirds as before, coating all sides with sugar. Chill for 30 minutes then roll again, coat with sugar and fold, then chill for 30 minutes.

Roll the pastry out to a 1 cm (½ in) thickness. Cut it in half, then fold the corners of the dough to meet in the centre. Place the two pieces of dough in buttered cake tins, pressing slightly so the dough fits the tins snugly. Cover the cake tins with a towel and leave to rise for 2 hours in a warm place.

Bake in a preheated oven at 200°C (390°F/Gas 6) for about 30 minutes, then carefully turn out onto a rack. The cake will be beautifully caramelised. Cut into wedges.

SERVES 12-16

RUM SAVARIN

Savarin au rhum
From the Lorraine Region

---

1 x 7–10 g (⅓–¼ oz) sachet dry yeast

50 ml (2 fl oz) warm milk

200 g (7 oz) plain (all-purpose) flour, sifted

3 large eggs, at room temperature

90 g (3 oz) unsalted butter, slightly softened

345 g (12 oz/1½ cups) sugar

500 ml (17 fl oz/2 cups) water

zest of 1 lemon

75 ml (2½ fl oz/¼ cup) rum

1½ cups (170 g/6 oz) whipped cream

400 g (14 oz) raspberries

The savarin, a yeast cake moistened with a rum-flavoured sugar syrup, is one of the great French gâteaux and a favourite of mine. Baking this recipe will need a little experience with using yeast.

Dissolve the yeast in the warm milk.

In the bowl of an electric beater fitted with a beating attachment, place the flour, the yeast and milk mixture, and the eggs and beat for about 2 minutes until the mixture is elastic. If you do not have an electric beater, beat it with a wooden spoon. Cover with a cloth and allow to rise for about 1 hour.

Lightly butter a 20 cm (7 in) ring cake tin. Preheat the oven to 200°C (390°F/Gas 7).

Add the softened butter and 1 tablespoon sugar to the risen dough and beat thoroughly with a wooden spoon. Place the mixture in a piping bag without a nozzle and pipe into the prepared tin, tapping the tin lightly to eliminate any air bubbles. Leave to rise uncovered for 30 minutes in a warm place, then bake in the preheated oven for 25 minutes.

In a saucepan, bring the water, remaining sugar and lemon zest to the boil and cook for 5 minutes.

When the cake is cooked, remove from the oven and wait about 3 minutes before turning it out onto a dish.

Stir the rum into the sugar syrup and pour this slowly over the cake. Allow the cake to absorb the syrup.

Serve the cake garnished with whipped cream and raspberries.

SERVES 6-8

CHERRY & HAZELNUT CAKE

Gâteau aux cerises et aux noisettes
From the Limousin Region

⋯

150 g (5 oz) butter, cut into small pieces
150 g (5 oz) caster sugar
zest of 1 lemon, finely grated
3 eggs, at room temperature
150 g (5 oz) self-raising flour
3 tablespoons almond meal
80 g (3 oz) skinned roasted hazelnuts, each crushed into 2–3 pieces
about 30 large cherries, pitted
2 tablespoons extra caster sugar
2 tablespoons smooth apricot jam, heated

The texture and flavour of the cherries are fabulous in this delicious cake, and if you own a cherry pitter that will make things so much easier. It's best to eat this cake within 24 hours of making it – but that shouldn't be too difficult!

Preheat the oven to 180°C (350°F/Gas 4). Butter and flour a 22 cm (8 in) loose-based cake tin.

Using an electric beater, cream the butter, sugar and lemon zest for a few minutes until light and creamy.

Add the eggs one at a time to the creamed butter and beat well. Then on low speed carefully add the self-raising flour, almond meal and roasted hazelnut pieces, beating until just mixed.

Carefully pour the mixture into the prepared tin and flatten the top with a spatula. Press the pitted cherries about 5 mm (¼ in) into the mixture, keeping them about 1 cm (⅓ in) away from the sides of the tin. Dust the top with the extra caster sugar.

Bake in the preheated oven for about 50 minutes until the cake is cooked.

Remove the cake from the oven and rest it for 15 minutes before carefully turning it out onto a cake rack. Brush the top of the cake with the heated jam and allow the cake to cool before serving.

It's delicious served with cream or ice cream.

SERVES 8

CRUNCHY ALMOND BISCUITS OF CORDES

Les croquants de Cordes
From the Albi/Midi-Pyrénées Region

250 g (9 oz) caster sugar
2 egg whites
140 g (5 oz) plain (all-purpose) flour
180 g (6 oz) whole almonds, halved
½ teaspoon natural vanilla essence
icing sugar for dusting

Cordes, located near the stunning town of Albi, is one of the most beautiful hilltop villages in France and one of my favourite French destinations. This unique biscuit was created at the end of the 19th century.

In a bowl, combine the sugar with the egg whites and whisk until creamy white. Then mix in the flour, almonds and vanilla essence until just combined. Form the dough into a ball, wrap in plastic wrap, flatten it down to about 2 cm (¾ in) thick and refrigerate for an hour.

Preheat the oven to 200°C (390°F/Gas 7). Lightly grease a biscuit tray.

Roll the dough out to a 1 cm (⅓ in) thickness (do this between two sheets of baking paper) and cut into strips 8 cm (3 in) wide, then cut each strip into 2 cm (¾ in) pieces. Do not be concerned if the biscuits are slightly different sizes. Place the biscuits on the greased biscuit tray.

Bake the biscuits in the preheated oven for about 8 minutes or until dry. When cold, dust lightly with icing sugar.

These are lovely served with fresh seasonal fruits, especially peaches, apricots and raspberries. I also like them with baked figs.

MAKES 25-30 BISCUITS

DUTCH COCOA MOUSSE SLICE WITH GINGERBREAD

Mousse au cacao en millefeuille
de pain d'épices
From the Northern France/Holland Region

---

1 loaf of Dutch gingerbread
200 g (7 oz) quark (smooth, fresh, low-fat, unripened cheese)
30 g (1 oz) Dutch cocoa powder (unsweetened)
3 eggs, separated
3 tablespoons caster sugar
a pinch of cream of tartar
icing sugar for dusting
12 chocolate sticks flavoured with orange (optional)

It has become fashionable in France over the last 10 years for chefs to use pain d'épices (Dutch gingerbread) in ice creams, mousses and custards. I serve it like a millefeuille with chocolate mousse for the filling.

Using a serrated knife, cut 18 slices of gingerbread about 5 mm (¼ in) thick.

Place the quark and cocoa powder in a bowl and whisk until combined. Add the three egg yolks and half the sugar and beat until smooth.

Place the egg whites in a bowl with the cream of tartar and, using an electric beater, beat into stiff peaks. Add the remaining caster sugar and continue beating until smooth.

Mix a little of the beaten egg whites into the cocoa mixture, then gently fold in the remaining egg whites and mix until just combined.

Place six slices of gingerbread on a large dish. Top each with 1 tablespoon cocoa mousse, then with a second slice of gingerbread. Add another spoonful of mousse and finish with a slice of gingerbread. Spread a little extra mousse on the sides of the small cakes and dust the top with icing sugar. Refrigerate for at least 1 hour before serving.

Garnish each slice with two chocolate sticks.

SERVES 6

NOUGAT CAKE FROM TOURS

Nougat de Tours
From the Central Loire Valley Region

400 g (14 oz) sweet shortcrust pastry
60 g (2 oz) apricot jam
150 g (5 oz) diced confit fruits (3 or 4 varieties)
80 g (3 oz) ground almond
80 g (3 oz) caster sugar
3 egg whites
a pinch of cream of tartar
icing sugar for dusting

This lovely speciality from the Loire Valley town of Tours is actually not nougat but a cake filled with confit fruits and a type of almond meringue called macaronade (macaron mixture).

Preheat the oven to 200°C (390°F/Gas 7).

Roll the pastry out thinly and line a 20 cm (8 in) loose-based flan (tart) tin. Spread the base of the pastry with apricot jam and cover with the confit fruits.

Mix the ground almond with the caster sugar and sift together.

Beat the egg whites and cream of tartar into stiff peaks, then gently fold in the ground almond and sugar preparation. Spread this on top of the confit fruits, finishing just short of the pastry edges. Smooth the top with a spatula.

Generously dust the top with icing sugar. Bake in the preheated oven for about 30 minutes until the pastry has browned and is cooked. Cool before serving.

SERVES 8

DESSERTS
& TARTS

CORSICAN CHEESE CAKE

Fiadone Corse
From the Island of Corsica

500 g (1 lb 2 oz) fresh brocciu cheese (or ricotta or ewe's milk ricotta)
200 g (7 oz) caster sugar
zest of 1 lemon, finely grated
2 tablespoons lemon juice
1 tablespoon alcohol of your choice (grappa is nice)
5 x 60 g (2 oz) eggs, room temperature

This popular Corsican family cake is made with brocciu, a fresh ewe's milk cheese that resembles ricotta but is a bit stronger in flavour.

Place the fresh cheese in a muslin cloth over a colander or bowl and refrigerate for 1 hour to drain off the excess liquid.

Preheat the oven to 180°C (350°F/Gas 4). Butter a 20 cm (8 in) cake tin.

Take the drained cheese out of the refrigerator.

Combine the cheese with 50 g (2 oz) caster sugar and the lemon zest in a bowl. Stir until smooth, then mix in the lemon juice and alcohol.

In another bowl, whisk the eggs with the remaining sugar for about 5 minutes until foamy. Slowly whisk the cheese preparation into the eggs, beating until the texture is creamy.

Transfer the mixture to the prepared cake tin and bake in the preheated oven for about 45 minutes.

Allow to cool before turning out.

It's lovely served with fresh berries and dusted with sugar.

SERVES 8-10

RHUBARB & RASPBERRY GRATIN

*Gratin à la rhubarbe
et aux framboises*
From the Picardy Region

1 kg (2 lb 3 oz) rhubarb
50 g (2 oz) butter, melted
50 g (2 oz) sugar
2 cups (250 g/8½ oz) raspberries
2 tablepoons orange juice
2 tablepoons finely grated lemon zest
2 egg yolks
1 cup (110 g/3½ oz) whipped cream
icing sugar for dusting

Many French people living in rural areas in the north grow fruit trees, berries and rhubarb. This easy dessert is sure to please everyone.

Preheat the oven to 180°C (350°F/Gas 4). Butter six individual gratin dishes.

Trim the rhubarb and peel away the hard skin. Cut the rhubarb into about 5 cm (2 in) pieces. In a bowl, toss the rhubarb with the melted butter and then with the sugar.

Place the rhubarb neatly in an ovenproof dish and bake in the preheated oven for about 10 minutes until the rhubarb is soft. Transfer the rhubarb to the six gratin dishes and fill the gaps with a few raspberries.

Combine the orange juice, lemon zest and egg yolks in a bowl. Place the bowl over a saucepan of almost simmering water and whisk the yolks continuously until the preparation is creamy and light. It takes a few minutes.

Remove the bowl from the heat and gently fold in the whipped cream.

Spread the egg and cream mixture over the top of the fruit and dust with icing sugar.

Place under a hot grill until the top becomes golden. Serve immediately.

SERVES 6

ROAST FIGS WITH CARAMELISED NUTS

Figues rôties aux noix caramélisées
From the Rhône Valley Region

6 large ripe figs
30 g (1 oz) butter
½ star-anis
2 tablespoons sugar
12 walnut halves
12 roasted hazelnuts
12 almonds, halved
20 grapes
4 tablespoons pouring cream

The Rhône Valley, well known for its fruity red wines, enjoys plenty of sunshine and the local figs are sweet and juicy. This luscious dessert is a cinch to make, but take care not to burn yourself with the caramelised nuts.

Cut the figs into quarters.

Heat the butter in a large frying pan. Add the star-anise and the figs and cook for 3–4 minutes on a medium heat, turning the figs gently.

Transfer the figs to four plates, arranging them attractively. Leave the star-anise in the pan.

Add the sugar to the pan and stir, lightly caramelising the sugar. Add the walnuts, hazelnuts, almonds and grapes and stir for 2 minutes. Add the cream and mix well to obtain a sauce texture.

Spoon the nuts and grapes around and over the figs.

It's lovely served with vanilla ice cream.

SERVES 4

BLACKCURRENT & ALMOND CLAFOUTIS

Clafoutis au cassis et aux amandes
From the Burgundy Region
by Pierrick Boyer

225 g (8 oz) creamed cottage cheese or quark (in France it is called fromage frais (smooth, low-fat, unripened fresh cheese)

4 egg yolks

30 g (1 oz) cornflour (cornstarch)

250 g (8½ oz) caster sugar

200 g (7 oz) ground almond

2 cups (250 g /8½ oz) blackcurrants, fresh or frozen

icing sugar for dusting

8 scoops vanilla ice cream (or a flavour of your choice)

Blackcurrants, or as the French say cassis, are plentiful in Burgundy. Clafoutis is a type of pudding made with fruits. It's easy to make and a perfect family dessert.

Preheat the oven to 160°C (320°F/Gas 2).

In a large bowl mix the cottage cheese with the egg yolks and cornflour. Stir in the caster sugar and ground almond. Transfer the mixture to a piping bag and pipe into eight individual porcelain baking dishes.

Dot the top with blackcurrants and bake in the preheated oven for about 20 minutes.

Remove from the oven and allow to cool a little.

Dust with icing sugar and serve with vanilla ice cream.

SERVES 8

STRAWBERRY TART

Tarte aux fraises
From the Loire Valley Region

❧ ──── ⁘ ────

a little plain (all-purpose) flour
400 g (14 oz) sweet shortcrust
pastry
300 ml (10 fl oz) crème fraîche
1 tablespoon cointreau
2 tablespoons milk
2 tablespoons icing sugar
2 punnets of strawberries, hulled,
washed and halved
4 tablespoons smooth apricot jam
3 tablespoons peeled pistachio
nuts, cut into small pieces

This dessert takes me back to my youth in my native Loire Valley. In summer, my father grew large quantities of strawberries in our family garden and my mum and grandmother made beautiful fruit tarts.

Preheat the oven to 180°C (350°F/Gas 4). You will need a 25 cm (9 in) loose-based flan (tart) tin.

Dust the bench with plain flour and roll the pastry out thinly to about 4 mm (⅕ in).

Line the flan tin with the pastry and cover it with foil. Top the foil with pastry weights to stop the pastry from shrinking during cooking. Bake the pastry in the preheated oven for about 20 minutes.

In a bowl, beat the crème fraîche with the cointreau and milk until almost firm. Add the icing sugar and mix well. This is called a 'chantilly cream'.

Spread the chantilly cream over the cooled pastry shell. Top gently with strawberry halves and brush the berries lightly with apricot jam. Sprinkle pistachio nuts around the edge of the tart and refrigerate until ready to slice and serve.

SERVES 8

PEAR & ALMOND TART

Tarte Bourdalou
From the Paris Region
by Pierrick Boyer

PASTRY
160 g (5½ oz) plain (all-purpose) flour
120 g (4 oz) butter
50 g (2 oz) caster sugar
¼ teaspoon salt
2 egg yolks

ALMOND CREAM
50 g (2 oz) butter
50 g (2 oz) ground almond
50 g (2 oz) caster sugar
2 large eggs
50 ml (2 fl oz) pouring cream
3 large pears, poached, cored and each cut into 6 segments
icing sugar for dusting

Many Parisian families buy this popular French dessert from the local patisserie but it is fun to make at home. The almond cream goes beautifully with the poached pears.

Butter a 25 cm (10 in) loose-based flan (tart) tin.

To make the pastry, mix together the flour, butter, caster sugar and salt in the bowl of an electric beater. Lastly, beat in the 2 egg yolks.

Form the dough into a ball, cover it in plastic wrap and place in the refrigerator to rest for at least 1 hour.

Preheat the oven to 160°C (320°F/Gas 2).

Roll the pastry thinly and line the tart tin. Trim the edges of the pastry then place the tin in the freezer for a few minutes.

To make the almond cream, mix the butter with the ground almond, caster sugar and the eggs in a blender. Lastly, mix in the cream.

Spread the almond cream over the pastry shell and then arrange the segments of poached pears on top.

Bake in the preheated oven for at least 20 minutes or until the pastry is cooked and browned. Allow to cool.

Dust the tart with icing sugar and remove it from the tin.

SERVES 8

BLUEBERRY TART

Tarte aux myrtilles
From the French Alps Region

2 egg yolks
50 g (2 oz) caster sugar
25 g (1 oz) plain (all-purpose) flour
250 ml (8½ fl oz/1 cup) milk
⅓ vanilla pod, slit lengthways
200 g (7 oz) block ready-made puff pastry, thawed
2 tablespoons thickened cream, whipped and chilled
250 g (8½ oz/2 cups) fresh blueberries
2 extra tablespoons caster sugar
icing sugar for dusting
6 dollops of thick (heavy) cream
a few mint leave

The French adore to serve fruit tarts for a special family occasion. It's great to bake your own rather than buying one from a pastry shop as beautiful fresh fruits are so readily available.

I like to make this tart in a loose-based rectangular flan (tart) tin about 30 cm (12 in) long.

Preheat the oven to 200°C (390°F/Gas 6).

Cream the egg yolks with the caster sugar in a bowl, then mix in the plain flour.

In a small saucepan, heat the milk with the vanilla pod to almost boiling point.

Add the hot milk to the egg yolk preparation and mix, then transfer this to a saucepan and cook on medium heat until it thickens. Return the preparation to the bowl, whisk for 10 seconds and allow to cool.

Roll out the puff pastry to a thickness of about 3 mm (⅛ in) and to measure about 35 cm (14 cm) x 15 cm (6 in). Lift the pastry and line the base and sides of the rectangular tin.

Mix the cooled, whipped cream into the cold custard and spread it over the base of the pastry. Garnish the top with blueberries and sprinkle with the extra caster sugar. Trim the edges of the pastry.

Bake the tart in the preheated oven for about 40–45 minutes or until the pastry is cooked and browned.

Remove the tart from the oven and allow to cool.

Slice the tart into six portions. Dust with icing sugar and garnish with a dollop of cream and a few mint leaves.

SERVES 6

PEACHES & APRICOTS POACHED IN JURANÇON WINE

*Verrine de pêches et abricots
au vin de Jurançon*
From the Béarn/Pyrénées Region

4 apricots

4 peaches

250 ml (8½ fl oz/1 cup) fresh orange juice

115 g (4 oz/½ cup) sugar

150 ml (5 fl oz) sweet Jurançon wine or another sweet wine

200 ml (7 fl oz) thickened (whipping) cream

3 tablespoons sweetened chestnut cream (*crème de marrons*)

2 tablespoons toasted flaked almonds

icing sugar for dusting

In France in the last few years, chefs have been serving this delightful summer dessert in glasses. The French word for glass is 'verre' which is why this dessert is called a 'verrine'. It's a refreshing way to finish a rich meal.

Wash and halve the apricots and peaches and remove the stones. Quarter the peaches.

Heat the orange juice, sugar and sweet Jurançon wine in a saucepan and add the apricots and peaches. Stir gently, bring to a simmer and poach the fruits for about 15 minutes or until soft.

Transfer to a bowl and allow to cool, then cover with plastic film and refrigerate.

Whip the cream until firm. Gently combine the whipped cream with the chestnut cream, then transfer to a piping bag fitted with a serrated nozzle.

Carefully spoon the cold fruit into four glasses and pipe some chestnut cream on top of the fruit. Refrigerate if not serving immediately. Just before serving, sprinkle the top with toasted flaked almonds and dust with icing sugar.

SERVES 4

POACHED PEACHES WITH STRAWBERRIES & SPARKLING VOUVRAY SAUCE

*Pêches pochées sauce aux fraises
et au Vouvray pétillant*
From the Tours/Loire Valley Region

---

6 lovely ripe peaches
500 ml (17 fl oz/2 cups) water
400 g (14 oz) sugar
½ vanilla pod, slit lengthways
3 tablespoons whipped cream
500 g (1 lb 2 oz) strawberries,
hulled (wild strawberries are
excellent)
125 ml (4 ½ fl oz/½ cup) sparkling
vouvray wine
3 tablespoons peeled pistachio
nuts, finely chopped

The region around the Loire is often referred to as the 'garden of France' because fruits and vegetables grow very well in the mild climate. This simple recipe is traditionally made with the delicious local sparkling wine, vouvray.

Gently drop the peaches into a saucepan of boiling water and cook for 1 minute. Drain the peaches and peel them carefully.

Bring to the boil, in a medium saucepan, 2 cups water with 350 g (12 oz) of the sugar and the vanilla pod. Add the peeled peaches and simmer for about 10 minutes. Allow the peaches to cool in the syrup.

In a bowl, whisk the remaining sugar and the whipped cream.

Blend the strawberries into a coarse purée. Fold the strawberries and the sparkling wine into the cream and refrigerate until needed.

Place the drained peaches in a serving bowl. Spoon the strawberry sauce over the fruit, sprinkle with pistachio nuts and serve.

SERVES 6

CHOCOLATE & HAZELNUT ICE CREAM CAKE

Glace au chocolat et aux noisettes
From the Alps/Italian Border Region

5 egg yolks
200 g (7 oz) caster sugar
500 ml (17 fl oz/2 cups) hot milk
2 teaspoons bitter cocoa powder
100 g (3½ oz) dark chocolate,
cut into small pieces
1½ cups (170 g/6 oz) whipped
cream
2 tablespoons water
3 drops red wine vinegar
100 g (3½ oz) roasted hazelnuts
16 Italian biscuits; e.g. sfoliatine
or savoiardi

The Italian influence is strong in this Alps region. This ice cream cake is ideal for a special dinner party as it can be prepared in advance. You need an ice cream maker to prepare this dessert.

Beat the egg yolks in a bowl with 150 g (5 oz) of the caster sugar for about 5 minutes until light and pale.

Stir in the hot milk, then transfer to a saucepan and cook on medium heat without boiling, stirring with a wooden spoon until the custard lightly coats the spoon. Transfer the preparation to a bowl and stir in the cocoa powder and chocolate pieces. Allow to cool.

When cold, fold in 1 cup of the whipped cream, then churn the preparation in an ice cream maker.

While the ice cream is churning, place 50 g (2 oz) caster sugar, 2 tablespoons water and the red wine vinegar in a small saucepan. Bring to the boil and cook until it caramelises. Stir in the hazelnuts until the nuts are well coated.

Transfer the hazelnuts to a tray lined with baking paper. After 2 minutes or so, crush about half of the hazelnuts (this can be done between two layers of baking paper using a rolling pin) and add the crushed nuts to the churning ice cream.

Transfer the firm ice cream to a mould, cover and place in the freezer for a few hours.

To unmould, dip the mould in warm water and turn the ice cream out onto a cold platter.

Pipe a little of the remaining whipped cream around the sides of the ice cream and attach the biscuits to the sides. Decorate the top with the remaining cream and the whole caramelised hazelnuts.

SERVES 8

ROLLED SAVOY SPONGE WITH BLUEBERRIES

Biscuit de Savoie roulées aux myrtilles

From the Alps/Savoie Region

3 eggs, separated, at room temperature

zest of 1 lemon, grated

150 g (5 oz) caster sugar

a pinch of cream of tartar

45 g (1½ oz) plain (all-purpose) flour

45 g (1½ oz) cornflour (cornstarch)

3 tablespoons brandy

200 g (7 oz) blueberry jam

100 g (3½ oz) toasted flaked almonds

icing sugar for dusting

The Biscuit de Savoie is a regional sponge cake that is very popular for celebrating family birthdays and name days. Wild blueberries are plentiful in the Alps and so the sponge is rolled with blueberry jam.

Preheat the oven to 180°C (350°F/Gas 4).

Butter a 36 cm (14 in) x 26 cm (10 in) Swiss roll tin (jelly roll tin) and line it with baking paper. Butter and flour the baking paper.

Place the egg yolks, lemon zest and half the sugar in the bowl of an electric mixer and beat until foamy.

In a separate bowl, add the cream of tartar to the egg whites and whisk into firm peaks. Gradually whisk in the remaining sugar until well incorporated.

Gently fold the egg whites into the beaten yolks. Sift together the plain flour and the cornflour and then fold into the egg preparation. Avoid over-mixing the flour. Pour the mixture into the prepared tin and spread to the edges.

Bake in the preheated oven for about 8 minutes or until firm to the touch.

Turn the warm sponge out onto a clean tea towel. Peel off the baking paper and roll the sponge up by gradually lifting the tea towel. Set aside to cool.

Unroll the sponge, sprinkle it with the liqueur and spread three-quarters of the jam over the sponge. Carefully roll up the sponge firmly.

Brush the remaining jam over the roll and refrigerate if not serving immediately.

Sprinkle with toasted almonds, dust with icing sugar and serve.

SERVES 10

COFFEE PARFAIT WITH PRUNES IN ARMAGNAC

*Parfait au café et aux
pruneaux à l'Armagnac*
From the South West Region

15 prunes, pitted and halved
50 ml (2 fl oz) armagnac
200 g (7 oz) caster sugar
125 ml (4 ½ fl oz/½ cup) water
6 egg yolks
2 teaspoons coffee essence
1¼ cups (140 g/5 oz) whipped cream

Armagnac is a wonderful spirit made from grapes and matches very well with the prunes. Pay attention not to over-cook the sugar syrup or you'll have to start again.

Place the prunes and armagnac in a bowl, stir well and leave to macerate for at least 1 hour.

Heat the sugar and water in a small saucepan. Bring to a simmer and cook until the sugar syrup takes on a slight yellow tinge.

Place the egg yolks in the bowl of an electric beater and, while beating on medium heat, pour the sugar syrup in bit by bit over a period of about 20–30 seconds. Continue beating for about 10 minutes until it's creamy and cold.

Gently mix in the macerated prunes and coffee essence, then fold in the whipped cream. Transfer to a mould, cover with plastic film and freeze for at least 8 hours.

To unmould, dip the mould briefly in warm water and then turn out the parfait onto a platter.

It is lovely garnished with crystallised violets and, if you wish, a few extra prunes soaked in armagnac.

SERVES 8

APRICOT ICE CREAM WITH CARAMELISED ALMONDS

Glace à l'abricot aux amandes caramélisées

From the Northern Provence Region

1 kg (2 lb 3 oz) apricots
230 g (8 oz/1 cup) caster sugar
125 ml (4½ fl oz/½ cup) orange juice
½ vanilla pod, slit lengthways
juice of 1 lemon
½ cup (56 g/2 oz) whipped cream
2 tablespoons water
3 drops red wine vinegar
1 cup (155 g/5½ oz) almonds
½ cup (56 g/2 oz) extra whipped cream

The northern Provence countryside has hills dotted with vineyards, olive and almond trees, and trees producing a variety of stone fruits. It is a place of great beauty.

Wash the apricots and remove the stones. Place the fruit in a saucepan with half the caster sugar, the orange juice and vanilla pod. Cover with a lid and simmer until the apricots are soft. Discard the vanilla pod and blend the apricots and liquid to a fine purée. Strain the purée into a bowl and allow to cool.

Add the lemon juice to the purée and fold in the whipped cream. Transfer the preparation to an ice cream maker and churn until done. Transfer to a mould, cover with plastic film and place in the freezer.

In a saucepan, heat the 2 tablespoons water, the remaining caster sugar and the vinegar. Bring to the boil and cook until lightly caramelised. Add the almonds and stir with a wooden spatula for 1–2 minutes until the almonds are well coated with dark caramel.

Place the caramelised almonds on a lightly oiled square of baking paper and leave to cool. Cut the cooled almonds into small pieces.

To unmould, dip the mould briefly in warm water and turn out the ice cream onto a cold platter.

Decorate the ice cream with the almond pieces and the extra whipped cream and serve.

SERVES 6-8

BELGIAN CHOCOLATE MOUSSE WITH RASPBERRIES

Mousse au chocolat Belge et framboises
From the Northern France/Belgium
Region

2 tablespoons pouring cream
200 g (7 oz) dark cooking
chocolate, cut into pieces
4 egg yolks
6 egg whites
a pinch of cream of tartar
1 tablespoon caster sugar
1½ cups (170 g/6 oz) whipped
cream
500 g (14 oz) raspberries

Chocolate mousse is one of the most popular desserts in the world. It's easy to make and recently I've served it in elegant glasses topped with raspberries. Irresistible!

Place the cream and chocolate pieces in a bowl resting over a pan of simmering water (bain-marie) on medium heat and whisk until the chocolate melts and is smooth. Remove the bowl from the bain-marie and stir in the egg yolks.

Place the egg whites and a pinch of cream of tartar in a separate bowl and beat until fairly firm. Add the sugar and continue beating the whites into stiff peaks.

Using a whisk, gently incorporate a quarter of the beaten egg whites into the chocolate preparation, then carefully fold in the rest of the whites.

Spoon the mixture into a piping bag and pipe it into the glasses. Cover with plastic film and place in the refrigerator to set for at least 4 hours.

When ready to serve, pipe a little whipped cream on top of each mousse and garnish with raspberries.

SERVES 6

BLUEBERRY & CHERRY COUPE

Verrine de myrtilles et cerises
From the Alps Region

1 gelatine sheet (or 1 teaspoon powdered gelatine)

36 cherries, pitted

juice of 1 lemon

400 g (14 oz) blueberries

110 g (4 oz) caster sugar

2 egg yolks

1 tablespoon plain (all-purpose) flour

1 tablespoon finely grated lemon zest

250 ml (8½ oz/1 cup) hot milk

2 egg whites

1 small layer of sponge cake, 1 cm (⅓ in) thick, cut into 6 circles (using one of the serving glasses)

icing sugar for dusting

In winter, the stunning, snow-covered mountains of the French Alps have a magical atmosphere. In summer, it's great fun to harvest the wild forest berries and wander among the fruit trees that grow in the valleys.

Drop the gelatine sheet into a large bowl of cold water to soften it.

Meanwhile, place 30 of the pitted cherries in a saucepan with the lemon juice, blueberries and 40 g (1½ oz) of the caster sugar. Bring to a simmer, stir gently and cook for about 2 minutes. Transfer the fruit to a bowl to cool.

In a bowl combine the 2 egg yolks with 20 g (⅔ oz) sugar. Stir in the flour and grated lemon zest. Whisk in the hot milk, then pour the preparation into a saucepan and cook on low heat, stirring until it thickens. Transfer to a bowl and whisk in the drained gelatine sheet (or the powdered gelatine). Allow to cool.

Beat the egg whites with 25 g (1 oz) caster sugar until firm and shiny. Beat in an extra 25 g (1 oz) caster sugar, then gently fold this into the cold custard. This preparation is called a *crème chiboust*. Transfer the mixture into a piping bag.

Spoon a little red fruit and juice into each glass and top with the circle of sponge cake. Pipe a 3 cm (1 in) layer of *crème chiboust* and add a bit more fruit and juice.

Garnish with a whole cherry and dust with icing sugar.

SERVES 6

CHAMPAGNE JELLY WITH RED FRUITS

Gelée de champagne aux fruits rouges
From the Champagne Region
by Pierrick Boyer

4 gelatine sheets (or 1 x 7 g/¼ oz)
sachet powdered gelatine)
500 ml (17 fl oz/2 cups) French
champagne
juice of ½ lemon
4 tablespoons caster sugar
250 g (8½ oz) strawberries, hulled
100 g (3½ oz) blueberries
200 g (7 oz) raspberries (or
blackberries)
icing sugar for dusting

Made with French champagne, this jelly is a very special adult indulgence. It's nice at the end of a dinner party as it's light, fruity and … because it's champagne!

Drop the gelatine sheets in a large bowl of cold water to soften.

Pour ¾ cup (190 ml) champagne into a saucepan and mix in the lemon juice and sugar. Bring almost to simmering point, then remove from the heat.

Drain the softened gelatine sheets, squeezing them by hand to remove excess water, then add them (or add the powdered gelatine) to the warm champagne and mix until dissolved. Stir in the remaining champagne.

Carefully pour the preparation into attractive glasses and refrigerate for at least 2 hours or place in the freezer for about 15 minutes.

Wash the strawberries, cutting large ones into halves or quarters.

Garnish the top of the set jelly with strawberries, blueberries and raspberries. Dust with icing sugar and serve.

SERVES 6

GREEN CHARTREUSE ICED PARFAIT

Soufflé glacé à la Chartreuse verte
From the Alps Region
by Philippe Mouchel

250 ml (8½ oz/1 cup) milk
1 vanilla pod, slit lengthways
9 egg yolks
300 g (10½ oz) caster sugar
150 ml (5 fl oz) green chartreuse liqueur
1¾ cups (200 g/7 oz) whipped cream
a selection of red fruits or other fresh fruits
icing sugar for dusting

Tasting of exotic herbs and plants, green chartreuse is a unique liqueur. This adult-only dessert is popular, relatively easy to prepare and looks good served in whisky-style glasses.

In a medium saucepan heat the milk with the vanilla pod.

Beat the egg yolks with the caster sugar in a bowl for at least 1 minute until well combined. Whisk in the hot milk and transfer back to the saucepan. Cook on medium heat, stirring with a wooden spoon until the custard thickens just slightly and coats the spoon. The custard must not boil; otherwise it will curdle.

Transfer the custard to the bowl of an electric mixer and beat with the whisk attachment for about 10 minutes until it doubles in volume and has cooled.

Mix in 100 ml (3½ fl oz) of green chartreuse and fold in the whipped cream.

Pour a little of the remaining chartreuse into each glass and top with the parfait preparation. Place in the freezer for at least 6 hours.

Garnish the top of each parfait with a selection of red fruits and dust with icing sugar.

SERVES 10

CHERRY FRUIT SALAD WITH LANGUEDOC BRANDY

*Salade de cerises au marc
de Languedoc*
From the Languedoc Region

---

100 g (3½ oz) raspberries
100 g (3½ oz) strawberries, hulled
juice of 1 lemon
juice of 2 oranges
½ cup (115 g/4 oz) caster sugar
1 tablespoon eau de vie de marc
du Languedoc (grape brandy)
30 cherries
3 ripe peaches
3 tablespoons toasted flaked
almonds
icing sugar for dusting

The sunny region of Languedoc produces very sweet fruit, including grapes for wine and brandy, and delicious plump cherries. This easy fruit salad makes a perfect finish to a special dinner and looks stunning. Eau de vie de marc du Languedoc is a regional grape brandy.

Place the raspberries and strawberries in a blender with the lemon juice, orange juice and sugar and blend to a purée. Strain into a bowl and discard the raspberry seeds. Mix in the eau de vie de marc.

Pit the cherries and add them to the berry purée.

Wash the peaches, cut each into eight segments and add to the fruit salad.

Spoon the fruit salad into deep plates. Decorate with the toasted almonds and dust with the icing sugar.

SERVES 8-10

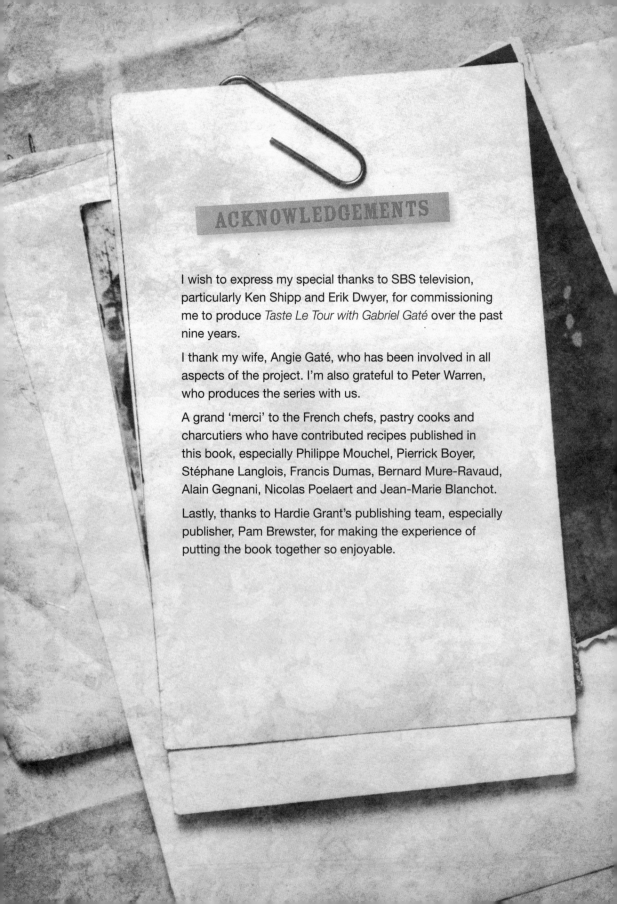

ACKNOWLEDGEMENTS

I wish to express my special thanks to SBS television, particularly Ken Shipp and Erik Dwyer, for commissioning me to produce *Taste Le Tour with Gabriel Gaté* over the past nine years.

I thank my wife, Angie Gaté, who has been involved in all aspects of the project. I'm also grateful to Peter Warren, who produces the series with us.

A grand 'merci' to the French chefs, pastry cooks and charcutiers who have contributed recipes published in this book, especially Philippe Mouchel, Pierrick Boyer, Stéphane Langlois, Francis Dumas, Bernard Mure-Ravaud, Alain Gegnani, Nicolas Poelaert and Jean-Marie Blanchot.

Lastly, thanks to Hardie Grant's publishing team, especially publisher, Pam Brewster, for making the experience of putting the book together so enjoyable.